SYBIL CAVANAGH grew up in Fife and is a graduate studying librarianship at the University of Wales Glasgow, and gained a Diploma in Scottish 1.... University. She came to West Lothian over twenty years ago, meaning to ... more than a few years, but married a local and has been happily settled ever since.

In 1990 she became librarian of the West Lothian Local History Library, and with evangelical zeal preaches the delights of local history and of West Lothian's heritage. She was a contributor to and joint organiser of *The Bathgate Book: a new history* (2001); and editor and joint author of *Pumpherston: the story of a shale oil village* (Luath Press, 2002); and has produced a series of local history booklets on subjects as diverse as grave-robbers, silver-mining, gypsies and foundlings.

A former chairman of the West Lothian History and Amenity Society, librarian of the West Lothian Family History Society, editor of the *West Lothian Heritage* newsletter and of the newsletter for Local Studies Librarians in Scotland, she is also a church organist (though not a very good one) and a gardener (ditto).

Blackburn: the Story of West Lothian's cotton and coal town

SYBIL CAVANAGH

Luath Press Limited

EDINBURGH

www.luath.co.uk

First Edition 2006

ISBN (10): 1-905222-40-8
ISBN (13): 978-1-9-0522240-7

A copy of this book on CD, showing sources of information and full references,
is available through the inter library loan system from West Lothian Local History
Library, Library HQ, Hopefield Road, Blackburn, West Lothian, EH47 7HZ.
Telephone 01506 776331.

The paper used in printing this product is recyclable. It is elemental chlorine free (ECF)
and manufactured from sustainable wood pulp forests. This paper and its manufacture
are approved by the National Association of Paper Merchants (NAPM), working towards
a more sustainable future.

Printed and bound by
Thomson Litho, East Kilbride

Typeset in 10.5 point Sabon

Acknowledgements

I am deeply grateful to the following people, both in Blackburn and beyond, without whose help this book could not have been written.

Staff of the National Archives of Scotland, the National Library of Scotland, Argyll and Bute Libraries, Argyll and Bute Archives, The Edinburgh Room, Glasgow University Archives and Business Records Centre, Glasgow City Archives, National Archives of Antigua, Paisley Museum and Art Galleries, the McLean Museum in Greenock, Scottish Mining Museum, Weslo Housing Management, Blackburn Area Housing Office, West Lothian Libraries Requests Service; and West Lothian Council Libraries for permission to reproduce many of the photographs in the West Lothian Local History Library.

David Anderson
Rev. Dr Robert Anderson
Andrina Baillie
Matt Campbell
Stephen Campbell
Violet Carson
William Cochrane
Colin Constance
Cheryl Drummond
Robert Dunlop
Evelyn Dunn
John Ewart
Stuart Eydmann
Jean Fooks
Maud Forsyth
Janette Fowlds
Linda Graham
Russell Hannah
David Hedges
Father Ryszar Holuka
W.T. Johnston
Eva Kennedy
Alison Kerr
Anne Kerr
John McCafferty

Sam McCartney
Graeme McGinty
John McLaren
Ronald McMillan
George McNeill
Margaret Meikle
W.I. Millan
John Miller
Owen Murdoch
Hamish Purdie
George Robertson
Jim Robertson
Councillor Willie Russell
St John's Church, Bathgate
Dr John Sheldon
Councillor Jim Swan
Robin Thompson
Sandy Thompson
Margaret Walker
Jim and Jean Wallace
Kirrie Whitton
Margaret Wilson
Lynne Wishart
Mary Wyper
Mr & Mrs Edward Younger

Particular thanks to Mrs Mary Wilson, the members of the Blackburn Young at Heart Group and Blackburn Church Men's Association; Jim Walker for his excellent memoir of growing up in Blackburn; Alex Russell who has done so much to ensure that Blackburn's history is not forgotten; Helen Scott and Elizabeth Henderson for very many comments, corrections and suggestions; and my husband Brian for his patience.

Crown copyright material is reproduced with the permission of the Controller of HMSO and Queen's Printer for Scotland.

Contents

Foreword

NO HISTORY OF A community can be written without a great deal of help and advice from local people. Many Blackburn people have given generously of their time, memories, knowledge, historical records and photographs. Though I work in Blackburn, surrounded every day by the recorded history of West Lothian in the county's Local History Library, I often felt during the writing of this book that I should have left the task to a native. However, the book is now finished for better or worse, and I ask forbearance for its inadequacies – for having to leave out so much that perhaps should have gone in, and perhaps for putting in some things that would have been better left out.

I decided to begin the present history in the late 18th century when Blackburn moved to its present site. Before that date, historical records are scarcer, not so readily available locally, and require more expertise and more spare time than I possess. The 245 years covered here took 11 years to research (with a few interruptions). Had I started in the medieval period, I might not have lived long enough to complete it. At any rate, the late 18th century saw the beginning of recognisably modern Blackburn and seems a good place to begin.

Introduction

THE HISTORY OF BLACKBURN has been a story of upheavals and constant change. It has had the unique distinction of twice being a New Town within a period of two hundred years.

In the 1770s, the old village of Blackburn was cleared away and a new settlement was created half a mile to the west. With the establishment of the Cotton Mill, the 'new town of Blackburn' became the first industrialised community in West Lothian. In the second half of the nineteenth century, cotton gave way to coal, but after a century, the coal industry too closed down.

As the coal industry declined, one of Scotland's largest factories was being built on the doorstep, and Blackburn doubled in size in its second incarnation as a New Town. Then once again came decay, when the closure of British Leyland brought deep social and economic problems. The growth of Livingston New Town within a few miles of Blackburn distorted the local economy, and contributed to ending the village's brief period of economic independence. But once again, Blackburn weathered the storm, and emerged as a new kind of community. Older Blackburn residents regret the disappearance of the old Blackburn in the 1960s; but Blackburn has been changing for years – constant upheavals every half-century or so have been the pattern throughout its history. And each time, the people have fashioned a new sort of community – different certainly, but workable.

Blackburn's history can also be seen as a microcosm of Scottish history. Its mansion house, built in the 18th century, was paid for by the profits of the sugar plantations of the West Indies – sugar being Britain's largest single import in the second half of the 18th century. Blackburn then flourished as a textile village, part of the enormous British cotton industry in the first half of the 19th century. Then came its period as a mining village, coinciding with the vital importance of coal mining to the British economy. The loss of the local coal mines was just part of the national decline of the industry; and the loss of the British Leyland factory reflected the failure of a well-meaning but ill-judged British government policy to move new industries to areas of declining heavy industry. The difficulties of the early 1980s were part of the serious economic depression which Scotland suffered at that period; and the village's current revival reflects the more cheerful economic scene in Scotland today.

But though typical of wider Scottish history, Blackburn's history is also unique. As the years go by, that heritage has a tendency to be forgotten. Already some local place names survive only in the memories of the oldest residents. The Cotton Mill is remembered, but the larger flax spinning and weaving mills at the other end of the village have been forgotten. These things must be recorded and passed on to the rising generation so that they can take pride in their heritage. Blackburn has had a difficult past, but it is one well worth remembering and celebrating.

CHAPTER I

A New Road, a New Laird
and a New Mansion

TWO EVENTS CONTRIBUTED TO a sea-change in the development of Blackburn village: the establishment of a turnpike road between Edinburgh and Glasgow, which passed through Blackburn; and the purchase of the estate of Blackburn by George Moncrieff.

The Great Toll Road

Until the mid eighteenth century, each parish was responsible for the upkeep of its own roads. Lack of money and of proper supervision meant that they were generally poorly built and badly maintained – muddy in winter, dusty and rutted in summer. Turnpike or toll roads were introduced as a solution to these difficulties, and Blackburn developed along the turnpike road of the 1760s.

The turnpike system resulted in a marked improvement in main roads. Landowners whose properties lay on or near the road, formed themselves by Act of Parliament into a Turnpike Trust. The Act gave the trustees powers to build a new road or upgrade existing roads, raising money by subscriptions or loans on the security of future tolls. Tollbars (turnpikes), where a gate obliged the traveller to stop, were built at intervals of no less than six miles along the route. The toll-keeper emerged from his tollhouse, and demanded payment according to a fixed scale of charges. On payment, a ticket was issued, the gate was opened, and the traveller went on his way. Certain categories of travellers were exempt: pedestrians, soldiers and clergymen on duty, church-goers and funeral-goers; certain farming activities, mail coaches – and the Royal family. All those in wheeled vehicles or driving herds of animals had to pay up. The benefit to the traveller was quicker, more comfortable travel on good roads; the benefit to the landowners was increased revenue as the general prosperity of their tenantry increased, and as trade and industry became established on their lands.

In West Lothian, the first road to be turnpiked was the main Edinburgh-Glasgow route via Linlithgow. In 1764 a turnpike trust was set up to establish a toll road from Edinburgh to Glasgow, via the southern route through Livingston, Blackburn, Whitburn and Kirk o' Shotts. A road through Livingston and Blackburn certainly existed before 1764, but it was not a road which could support heavy or long-distance traffic. Formation of the turnpike trust produced money to upgrade it, and increased the number of travellers, carters and coaches passing through Blackburn, with all the resultant possibilities of trade and custom. For Blackburn, the significance of the turnpike road was this: from being a country backwater, it found itself on one of the main arteries of travel and trade between Edinburgh and Glasgow.

A regular stagecoach service between Edinburgh and Glasgow began to operate on this road in 1765, and the important markets of Glasgow and Edinburgh became accessible to local farmers and producers.

One of the only two surviving tollhouses in West Lothian is on Blackburn's toll road – at Long Livingston on the stretch of Cousland Road now closed to traffic, between the Mill and the Toll roundabouts. The next toll bar after Long Livingston was some seven miles further on – Murraysgate Toll at the west end of Whitburn.

Redhouse Farm, originally built as the New Inn
Margaret Meikle

Two other important improvements were made in the vicinity of Blackburn within a few years of the turnpike road being built: by 1773, a New Inn had been established to serve travellers and stagecoaches. It survives today: the old, semi-derelict Redhouse Farmhouse. And in 1774, a bridge was built to carry the new road over the River Almond. It can still be seen at the west end of the village – the bridge which carries Mill Road over the river.

For the first few years, however, the village of Blackburn was not able to exploit the advantage of being on a turnpike road. For this to happen and for the village to develop, further changes were required.

George Moncrieff

In the late 1760s, the lands and Barony of Blackburn were owned by Mrs Elizabeth Baillie and her husband Captain John Lockhart Ross of Balnagown. (In Scotland, until the 19th century, married women generally kept their maiden names.) Captain Ross was a well-known figure in his day, a naval hero and captain of the Royal Navy ship, the *Tartar*. He became MP for Linlithgow Burghs in 1761, but was an absentee landlord of Blackburn, living mainly on his Easter Ross estate.

In 1768, Captain Ross sold the Barony of Blackburn to George Moncrieff. The minute of sale records the exact extent of the lands:

> all and haill the Lands and Barony of Blackburn, containing and comprehending the lands of Little Blackburn and houses, biggings, tenants, tenandrys and service of free tenants, parts, pendicles, apartinents thereof whatever, lying within the parish of Livingston, and Sheriffdom of Linlithgow. As also, all and haill the lands of Meikle Blackburn with the Miln thereof, Miln lands, multures, sucken and knaveship thereof... and likewise all and haill, the lands of Paddockshaw [Pottishaw] and houses, biggings, tenants, tenandrys and universal pertinents thereof, lying within the said parish of Livingston, shire of Bathgate; and sicklike all and haill the Lands of Torbane alias Trees, with houses, biggings, yards, parts, pendicles and pertinents thereof...

For these lands, George Moncrieff paid:

> the sum of eight thousand pounds stirling money as the agreed price and adiquate value of the forsaid Lands, teinds and others...

Of George Moncrieff, surprisingly little is known. He seems to have been of fairly humble Perthshire origins, not born into the nobility or gentry. In a legal deed, he is described as George Moncrieff 'sometime of the Island of Antigua, thereafter of London, and now of Airdrie.' As a young man, he went to the island of Antigua in the Caribbean (one of the Leeward Islands), and by 1750 was the owner of a sugar plantation called Rigby's and a sugar mill in the parish of St Mary's. Like John Newland, whose sugar fortune was bequeathed for the building of Bathgate Academy, Moncrieff owed his wealth to the labour of slaves. Having made his fortune, he came back to Britain, first to London, then to his native Scotland. There, like most men who had made their fortunes, he put his money into land. Land was the most secure form of investment, and also brought the important benefits of status, income and the entitlement to vote. After buying Blackburn, Moncrieff did not sell his Airdrie properties, but Blackburn became his home.

The exact date of George Moncrieff's acquisition of the Barony of Blackburn is not absolutely clear – nor was it even to his contemporaries. The minute of sale mentioned above gives the date of his entry to the property as Martinmas (November) 1768, but he is listed in the window tax register of 1769 as 'George Moncrieff in Blackburn' – which in 18th century terminology means he was the tenant, not the owner. Even his tenants were unsure of who their landlord was, as a 'Memorandum about the sale' records:

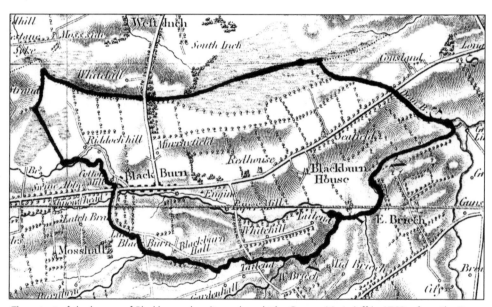

The extent of the barony of Blackburn when it was bought by George Moncrieff in 1768 – from the Dean Burn at Seafield in the east, to Riddochhill in the west. In addition, Moncrieff owned Pottishaw, Torbane and Trees which extended west to the Armadale-Whitburn road and almost as far north as Bathville.
Map surveyed by William Forrest, 1820
West Lothian Council Libraries

the other party [unidentified] had heard that Mr Moncrieff to whom Captain Ross had sold his estate, was in his own name warning out Tenants [i.e. giving them notice to quit], and doing other acts of property upon the estate which showed he was already in possession of it, and that there was actually a process pending between him and one of the Tenants for an ejection before the Sheriff of

the County. But they could learn nothing certain about it, till a few weeks thereafter when the Tenants bringing that process before the [Law] Lords, Mr
Moncrieff put his whole paper into Mr Crossbie's hands... who found that Mr
Moncrieff was really and truly in full possession of the Estate as he ever could be,
and this question betwixt Mr Moncrieff and the Tenants coming before the Court
of Session, they found that Mr Moncrieff had a right to turn them out.

It may be that George Moncrieff came first as a tenant in 1768, and afterwards
concluded his purchase of the property. Whatever the reason for the confusion,
he seems to have been in full and undisputed ownership by 1769.

The Barony of Blackburn

The 'intire and free Barony called the Barony of Blackburn' consisted of the lands
of Little Blackburn (i.e. Blackburnhall, south of the Almond) and Meikle Blackburn
(i.e. Riddochhill, Langdalehead, Faulheads, etc. – the land west of the Bathgate road).
In addition to this was what was generally known as the Mid Lot of Blackburn –
the mansion house and surrounding lands, comprising Seafield on the east side
and all the land as far as the Cross on the west, and including the Haugh and
Blackburn Mill. The barony also included some farms whose names are now lost
– Toar and Toshackbrae, and Whitehill and Tailend, both south of the Almond.

George Moncrieff was owner of the property for 29 years. Riddochhill,
Langdalehead and Faulheads (west of the Cross) were sold in 1788 to William
Honyman of Graemsay, and together with Pottishaw, Torbane and Trees, became
part of the estate of Torbanehill. Thereafter the estate of Blackburn comprised
some 670 acres, from Seafield Farm west to the Cross, and the annual rent
Moncrieff received from his farms was over £500.

Baronies

The term 'barony' means an administrative area. The owner of a barony held from the
Crown the right (or franchise) to administer justice by holding a barony court, presided over
by a baron bailie. The right was heritable – in other words it could be handed down from
father to son – until 1747, when heritable jurisdictions were abolished. Baronies continued
to exist, but in practice their rights of jurisdiction fell into disuse after 1747, because of the
growth of the state's power and the growing status and effectiveness of the sheriff courts,
the Court of Session and the High Court. After buying the Barony of Blackburn, George
Moncrieff is known to have appointed bailies to act as minor local agents, but in effect, the
term 'barony' meant little more than 'estate'.

Blackburn House. The design of the house was a little old-fashioned by the time it was built in 1772, and its architect is not known, as none of Moncrieff's estate papers survive.

Colin Constance

Blackburn House

What sort of mansion house existed when Moncrieff bought the estate, or exactly where it stood, is not clear. The hearth tax records of 1691 show that it had four hearths, and the window tax records of the 1760s show that it had only eight windows, so we can deduce that it was on a small and modest scale, probably two-storeyed and thatched. It is possible that it stood on the site of the present house, built by Moncrieff, and was demolished to make way for it.

Having decided that the gentle south-facing slope down to the River Almond was the right site for his new house, George Moncrieff began building soon after acquiring the estate. From window tax records, it can be deduced that it was built in 1772. Even when the house was newly built, four of its 37 windows were blocked up, presumably in order to avoid paying the window tax on them. A sales advertisement of 1792 described it as:

> a good modern Mansion-house of sixteen firerooms and closets, pigeon house, garden and complete set of offices [i.e. stables and steadings].

6

From the front, the house appears to be two-storeyed, but in fact an attic storey cuts across the upper windows. From the rear, the house is seen to be four storeys. The ground falls away to the south, allowing a basement storey to be accommodated. Inside are handsome rooms on the ground floor and first floor, with servants' quarters in the basement and attic. Two of the public rooms have fine Rococo plasterwork ceilings, and much of the woodwork survives.

Ptolemy Dean (later the consultant architect on the BBC television programme, *Restoration*) studied the house in 1990 and noted that:

> The contrast between the relief of the rather fine quality ashlar (at the windows and cornerstones) and the somewhat crude rubblestone would no doubt indicate that the rubble was originally harled (or rendered) in the traditional Scottish way.

The house was flanked by twin pavilions linked to the main house by curving walls. These pavilions were in fact barns, and behind them, hidden from public view, were more outhouses, steadings and a doocot. From the front, Blackburn House is a gentleman's residence; cleverly disguised is the fact that it was also a working farm. Of the two pavilions, only the east remains; the other has been demolished, as has the lodge house which used to stand at the gateway of the east drive. To the west and slightly to the south of the house was a walled garden, visible on maps and aerial photographs until the 1950s.

Blackburn before Moncrieff

When Moncrieff acquired the estate, the countryside around Blackburn looked very different from today. The land was not enclosed into fields; it was cultivated in rigs – narrow strips perhaps fifteen or twenty feet wide, separated by deep, wide ditches into which water drained and weeds, stones and rubbish were thrown. To the north was the boggy area of Easter Inch Moss, useless for anything except the digging of peats for fuel. The land of Blackburn was bleak, treeless, stony and infertile: ripe for improvement.

There was no village on the site of the present town of Blackburn. The road from Bathgate in those days took a route some half a mile to the east of the present Bathgate road, and joined the Great Toll Road approximately opposite the former Redhouse School. This brought the road close to the site of the *old* village of Blackburn.

Eighteenth century maps show that the old village of Blackburn lay across the road from Redhouse Farm. The map evidence is confirmed by a writer in the *West Lothian Courier* in 1877, who, in a long series of articles under the pen name of

Sylvester Sprightly, described every town and village in West Lothian, and its history. Of Blackburn, he had this to say:

> What was known as Blackburn formerly, occupied a different situation from the Blackburn of the present day. It stood a little to the west of Blackburn House and a large tree nearly opposite Redhouse, in the Cornielaw Park [marks the] site, which it once occupied. A part of it would extend into the field on the east side of the Cornielaw. It is about 120 years since the migration to its present site began.

Sylvester Sprightly was only about fourteen years out in his reckoning, and we may assume he was drawing his information from the older members of the community. This is the only written confirmation of the site of the old village, but it's likely that such major changes were still well known in 1877 to older people whose parents and grandparents had experienced them.

The village of Blackburn then was a fermtoun (farmtown), a cluster of poor thatched cottages occupied by tenants who farmed the land in common, along with some tradesmen/cottars (with rights to a little grazing land) and farm labourers; and, at least from 1760 on, a schoolmaster, Alexander Cuthbertson. From the subscription list of a book of poems published by Alex Cuthbertson in 1766, we know of the following residents of 'old' Blackburn – John Caldwall, mason; William Fliming, weaver; George Morton, smith; Thomas Steven, wright; and John Thornton, innkeeper. Perhaps John Thornton kept the New Inn, built to cater for the stagecoaches on the Great Toll Road. There were no streets in old Blackburn, no public buildings, no church, no shops, nothing that we associate with a village today. The only similar settlements in modern times are the townships of the Western Isles with their scattered crofts, whose old 'black-houses' are reminiscent of the houses in 18th century Lowland fermtouns. There may well have been other fermtouns on Moncrieff's Blackburn estate – Seafield, Little Blackburn, Latchbrae – which were also cleared, and at least some of their tenants moved to the new village.

Making Improvements

George Moncrieff was not a young man when he bought the Barony of Blackburn; he was in his late fifties. His marriage was childless, and his heir was his nephew, Thomas Clarkson. After his years abroad and several changes of residence, George Moncrieff evidently intended to settle down in Blackburn, because he at once began upon what his contemporaries would have termed 'improvements.'

He was an agricultural reformer, one of those active, innovative landowners who contributed to what is called the Agricultural Revolution. What is generally meant by this term is the great change that took place in farming between about 1750 and 1830. Agriculture began to be studied in a more scientific way, and great improvements were made in farming methods, animal breeding, crop rotations, and fertilisers. Trees were planted to provide shelter for crops and livestock. The land was drained and cleared of stones, the rigs were levelled and enclosed into large fields, bounded by hedges or walls. These fields were gathered together to make up large farms, run by one tenant farmer employing landless labourers. The countryside took on the appearance that is familiar today – the patchwork of regular enclosed fields, with plantations and belts of trees to beautify the land and protect it from gales. These changes formed a planned social and economic revolution, replacing subsistence-level farming with commercial farming for profit.

The main benefit of the changes was that the land became more fertile and was able to produce food for the population, which was growing at an immense rate. The drawback was that fewer people were required to work on the land. During these Lowland Clearances, many were cleared from the land altogether and had to move to towns and cities to find work, or even to emigrate; some who had once been small tenant farmers were reduced to labourers. The changes were necessary if agriculture was to keep pace with the growing population. The general standard of living went up, so that by the end of the eighteenth century, even labourers were better off than many tenants had been 50 years before.

The changes were generally initiated by the landowners, for only they had the knowledge of the new methods and the wealth to put them into practice. George Moncrieff was one of these reformers. He took a practical interest in his land, for instead of letting it all, and living purely as a gentlemen in his mansion house, he kept some of it in his own hands. It is likely that he did not set his own hand to the plough, but employed others to do the work under his supervision.

A certain amount of ruthlessness was necessary in an agricultural improver; even before it was realised that he had purchased the Blackburn estate, George Moncrieff had given some of his tenants notice to quit, a sure sign that he was enclosing the land. And within a year, or little more, he had begun to feu out the New Town – the present village of Blackburn.

CHAPTER 2

The Village that Flitted

AT THE TIME OF George Moncrieff's coming to Blackburn, the fermtoun consisted of a small number of households, and was situated only a few hundred yards from the spot Moncrieff had chosen for his new mansion – too close for 18th century notions of the distinction of ranks. He decided to move the village further away.

Too Close For Comfort

The idea of moving a whole village was not unfamiliar in the 18th century: the Duke of Argyll moved the old village of Inveraray from below the walls of the castle to its present site on the banks of Loch Fyne; and the Duke of Gordon knocked down Fochabers and rebuilt it further away from his castle. Once, peasants had huddled close to their lord's castle walls for protection; by the 18th century, the laird wished to keep his tenants at a respectful distance from his gates.

So George Moncrieff began to feu out small parcels of land three-quarters of a mile further to the west, on the north bank of the River Almond, and no doubt gave free stone, turf and thatch to assist in the building of houses in his 'New Town' of Blackburn. Sylvester Sprightly records that the 'new stance, when first occupied, had an uninviting appearance... covered with heather and whins, where now comfortable cottages and well-built houses and shops... are to be seen.' What had been unproductive land, when feued, became a source of income for George Moncrieff, as the new owners had to pay him feu duty annually.

Scotland's 18th Century New Towns

Town planning is not a 20th century innovation; the planning of villages either from scratch, or by the redesign of existing settlements, was practised in Scotland at least as early as the 17th century, and became the fashion for landowners in the second half of the 18th century. Between 1750 and 1830, it is estimated that some 180 villages were established or replanned in Scotland alone. One of these was Blackburn.

The English village, with its village green, manor house and ancient church, is almost unknown in Scotland, for the patterns of settlement in the two countries

Evidence of George Moncrieff's changes was recorded as early as 1773 in Armstrong's Map of The Three Lothians. To the west of Blackburn House is the old fermtoun of Blackburn, and the New Inn; and a little further to the west along the Great Toll Road, is the 'New Town', where the new village was beginning to take shape.

Trustees of the National Library of Scotland

evolved in very different ways. Until the beginning of the 18th century, the typical Scottish community was the fermtoun. Each parish would contain a number of these. English travellers, accustomed to neat, prosperous southern villages, customarily described Scottish fermtouns with scorn: 'miserable cabins' or even 'half a dozen dung-hills buried under the lee of a high bank.' Some larger and more prosperous villages existed in the Lowlands, such as Bathgate and Linlithgow, but they were generally burghs, protected and privileged commercial and market centres, whose status was conferred directly by the crown, or indirectly by the local baron. The trade privileges of the burghs in fact discouraged the general growth of villages; and remoteness, and lack of decent roads or transport, were further hindrances.

The planned village was just one of a wider range of improvements that were being undertaken throughout Lowland Scotland at the time – haphazardly, by individuals, not government, and in a piecemeal fashion. Agricultural improvements led to an increase in agricultural produce, for which a market had to be found, and a surplus of tenants and cottars, whose living was lost when their land was enclosed into new and larger farms. To both of these problems, a planned village offered a solution. But it was also a product of the thinking of the times, the idea that human behaviour could be shaped by the environment – the reordering of the farming landscape, and the planning of neat, pleasing villages. The partnership of agricultural improvements, a paternal landlord and improved roads was significant in the growth of many new towns in the late 18th century.

The object which the village-planner generally had in mind was to make money by attracting a greater number of inhabitants who would pay him rents or feu duties. There was also the hope of attracting manufacturing, the desire to beautify the estate, and perhaps the wish to improve the lot of the tenants, for whom most landlords seem to have felt at least some concern.

The New Site

The site of the new village of Blackburn was almost certainly chosen because of its closeness to the River Almond. Water, as well as being a necessity of life, was the power supply for 18th century industries such as grain, cotton and flax mills. The new site, three quarters of a mile to the west of the old, also had good transport links east, west, north and south. Straddling a busy main road, it would benefit from the custom of travellers.

At some point between about 1750 and 1773, the road from Bathgate to Blackburn was moved a few hundred yards to the west, to its present route. This was probably to bring it down to the new village, although it may have been dictated by agricultural improvements and changes to land use. At any rate, village tradition states that the first house in the new village was built at the foot of the (new) Bathgate road, and that the second one survives as a roofless ruin behind the Turf Hotel.

When a landowner feued his land, he in effect sold it, while retaining certain rights over it as feudal superior, including the right to receive an annual feu duty (a payment made by the purchaser every year to his feudal superior). The earliest known feuar of land in the New Town was James Hamilton, and another was Henry Davie, who feued from George Moncrieff in September 1770 'that pendicle or portion of land bounded on the West by the land feued to James Hamilton; on the South by the water, on the East by a Dyke to be run by him, and on the North by the Great High Road, consisting of one rood of ground with a dwelling House built thereon.' Another early feuar was John Wallace, first of a long dynasty of Blackburn masons. The new village is usually referred to in the Sasines as 'Newtown of Blackburn', or 'the village of New Blackburn.'

The feuing of land began slowly in the 1770s, but gained momentum in the 1780s and 1790s. A list of early feus would be of little use since their sites cannot always be accurately identified; but it is interesting to note that some of the names are those of residents of the old Blackburn – Caldwall, Dunlop, Hamilton, Thornton – who moved to the New Town, perhaps evicted by Moncrieff from their holdings in the old fermtoun. Some of the new names remained in the village for generations and may still have descendants there today – Davie, White, Wallace, Forrest, Lockhart,

West End, Blackburn, c.1900. On the right can be seen some of the original houses typical in the new village of Blackburn – single or double-storied, most of them thatched.

West Lothian Council Libraries

Duncan, Brownlee, Prentice, Edmiston, Purves, Bain, Turnbull, Lauder and Kidd. The occupations of the early feuars included carrier, wright, labourer, roadmaker, mason, shoemaker, cotton carder, and cotton spinner – mainly skilled workers; the more prosperous part of the community who could afford the cost of a feu.

Planning Blight?

The Sasine which records the sale to Richard Wallace of the piece of land in Bathgate Road on which the Masonic Hall is built is typical of the conditions laid down by the landowner, though in this case the land was feued not by George Moncrieff but by one of his successors, Thomas Douglas. The landowner's planning restrictions were almost as strict 200 years ago as the council's are today!

'One rood Scots land measure, having a front of eighty feet along the road from Blackburn to Bathgate, and extending backwards 173 feet... bounded ... on the south by a new Street to be formed of Thirty feet Broad to be called Kidd Street... any houses to be erected by the said Richard Wallace... should be five feet within the present hedge, and in a line with the house built by the said Alexander Kidd... three feet back from said street... should be covered with Tyles or Slates only.' Thatch was frowned upon (because of the fire risk) if slate could be afforded. As an incentive to take out a feu, the feuar was allowed to quarry stone free of charge from Thomas Douglas' quarries 'to the east of the Steam Engine.'

George Moncrieff in Old Age

By 1791, George Moncrieff was 80, a ripe old age for the time. Perhaps feeling his age, he put the Blackburn estate up for sale. The *Edinburgh Evening Courant* newspaper of 21 May 1791 carried the following advertisement:

George Moncrieff's signature
National Archives of Scotland

For sale by public roup at the Old Exchange Coffeehouse, Edinburgh – The Lands and Barony of Blackburn, in one or two lots as purchasers shall incline. These Lands lie 17 miles west from Edinburgh, the turnpike road from thence to Glasgow by Livingston, running thro' them. The Lands consist of about 670 acres Scots measure, and the yearly rent, after deducting public burdens, is £506 sterling. They are all inclosed and subdivided with hedges and stone dykes, and surrounded with very thriving plantations about 20 years old. The Lands are in high cultivation, are part in tenantry, and part in the proprietor's hands, viz. 300 acres, being in grass. Coal and lime are at present working in the lands, not included in the rental; also very fine iron stone, which promises to turn to great advantage.

The advertisement concludes with a brief description of the house, and mentions 'excellent Farm-houses for tenants. The Lands hold of the Crown, and entitle the proprietor to a vote in the County of Linlithgow.'

Evidently the estate did not find a buyer, or failed to reach a reserve price, for George Moncrieff tried again in the following year, but again failed to sell it. In this same year, he successfully disposed of his Lanarkshire estate, Loch of Auchinloch, for £5,200. Having failed to sell the whole Blackburn estate, he sold part of it – the West Lot – and leased another part – Seafield Farm – advertising it in the *Edinburgh Evening Courant* newspaper: '...lying on the great Glasgow road, two miles west from Livingston... upwards of 200 acres of good arable land... have been many years in the proprietor's own hands.' Other evidence of his improvements is given: '...excellent steading of Houses and Offices, fit to accommodate a Gentleman Farmer'. (This refers to Seafield Farm. There is also a mention of coal being worked on Seafield Farm.)

In 1796, 85 years old and doubtless aware that he was nearing the end of his life, Moncrieff handed over the estate of Blackburn to his nephew and heir, Thomas Clarkson, retaining only liferent of it. As well as the estate, he made over to his nephew 'all and sundry heritable and moveable property, debts and sums of money, goods, gear, effects, household furniture, bed and table linen... and plate of every kind...' This was done, the deed states in the usual phrase, because of 'the regard, favor and affection I have and bear to the said Thomas Clarkson.'

George Moncrieff continued to live at Blackburn in a modest style. According to tax records, he had neither carriage nor horses, but kept a manservant and a dog. His wife Catherine died on 2 July 1797, aged 82, and her gravestone can be seen in Livingston kirkyard, to the north of the church.

It is difficult, at this distance in time, to judge his character. In only one surviving document can his own voice be heard – a letter of condolence to a widow, Mrs Brown. The tone is dry and bracing rather than emotional, and was written soon after his move from Airdrie to Blackburn, when he was about 60. After a sentence or two about the mysterious ways of God's providence and resignation to His will, he continues:

> I never bore Mr Brown any ill will, but was resolved to break off all intimacy and connection in Business with him, after I found he was going on to ruin, and would not be advised. [This, to a woman who has just lost her husband, is scarcely tactful; and he continues:] I own too, that I began to dislike him, when I found he had no kind of regard or concern for his family, and in the latter part of my time at Airdrie, I avoided him as much as I could, and for that Reason was more seldom at Mavisbank; but I assure you, nothing I could ever observe in your conduct, had in the least altered the good opinion I always had of you.

Mrs Brown was asking for help in sorting out her husband's business affairs, and for advice on how she was to live. Moncrieff reluctantly agreed some limited response to the first request, but for the second, referred her instead to people who knew her circumstances and could better guide her. It may have been good advice, but it was probably not what she had hoped for. As far as can be judged from this one brief letter, Moncrieff was cool and businesslike; a man of probity, but more likely to inspire respect than affection. His involvement in slavery is abhorrent today, but the mid-18th century mind was only just beginning to recognise the inhumanity of such a practice. Trading in slaves was banned in 1807, but slavery was not abolished in Britain's colonies until 1833.

Summing up Moncrieff's achievements is difficult, since so little documentary evidence remains. He formed the modern day landscape of Blackburn and its surroundings, and comparison of Armstrong's 1773 map with Thomson's map of 1820 shows the extent of his changes. He 'rationalised' the land holdings and cleared some of his tenants and labourers from his land – ruthless measures, but perhaps necessary for farming to be modernised. He was in the vanguard of these changes in West Lothian. He seems to have taken no part in the public life of the county: he did not act as a Commissioner of Supply (forerunners of the county council), nor was he active as a heritor (the landowners in their role as church and school providers). He provided the impetus for the new town of Blackburn, but appears to have taken no steps to provide for employment. Perhaps because he had no long-standing connection with Blackburn, his interest in it was somewhat detached. But in the opinion of the writer of the Old Statistical Account, 'much praise is due to... Mr Moncrieff... for the great expense and unwearied application [he has] bestowed on improvements...'

George Moncrieff died in 1798, and Blackburn passed into the hands of his nephew, Major Thomas Clarkson.

CHAPTER 3

The Coming of the Cotton Mill

William Honyman of Graemsay

In 1788 another important figure in Blackburn's history emerges – William Honyman of Graemsay. He was a lawyer and advocate, the owner of lands in Sutherland and in Orkney (where the island of Graemsay is to be found), but his legal work lay chiefly in Edinburgh. He married the daughter of the notorious judge, Lord Braxfield, upon whom Robert Louis Stevenson based his character Weir of Hermiston, and who famously once said to the accused: 'Ye're a vera clever chiel, man, but ye wad be nane the waur o' a hanging.'

Lord Armadale

William Honyman is better known in the history of Armadale than in that of Blackburn. On the new Bathgate – Airdrie turnpike road (1792), a village began to grow up on the estate of Barbauchlaw, which William Honyman had bought in 1790. An inn had just been built when Honyman became one the Senators of the College of Justice (the judges who presided over the Court of Session, Scotland's supreme civil court), and took the legal title, Lord Armadale, after his estates in Sutherland. In compliment to him, the inn was named the Armadale Inn, and in due course the village too adopted this name.

In 1788, William Honyman had purchased from George Moncrieff the West Lot of the Barony of Blackburn, comprising Riddochhill, Langdalehead, and Fallhead in the parish of Livingston; Pottishaw in the parish of Whitburn; and also part of the lands of Torbane and the south half of Wester Inch. Riddochhill, Langdalehead and Fallhead were farms to the west of the Bathgate road and north of the Great Toll Road. Wester Inch lay a little to the north. So from 1788, the Blackburn estate of George Moncrieff had its boundary at the Bathgate road: west of the road was William Honyman's land.

On 24 June 1791, John Edmestone, labourer at Blackburn, bought a piece of ground from Honyman, and from then on, throughout the 1790s and early 1800s, Honyman continued to feu off portions of land at the west end, at a greater rate than ever George Moncrieff had done. Although he had a busy and successful legal career (aided by his father-in law's having become Lord Justice Clerk), and although he lived on his Lanark estate and not at Blackburn or Armadale, he appears to have been active in the management of his Linlithgowshire estates. So Blackburn is a village that owes its founding to two men – George Moncrieff and Lord Armadale. It's odd to think that Blackburn might with more reason be called Armadale, than Armadale itself!

Blackburn Cotton Mill

Blackburn Cotton Mill, the single most important factor in the development of Blackburn, was built in 1793. The previous chapter showed how the Agricultural Revolution affected local people. The story of Blackburn Cotton Mill shows how the Industrial Revolution affected the local area.

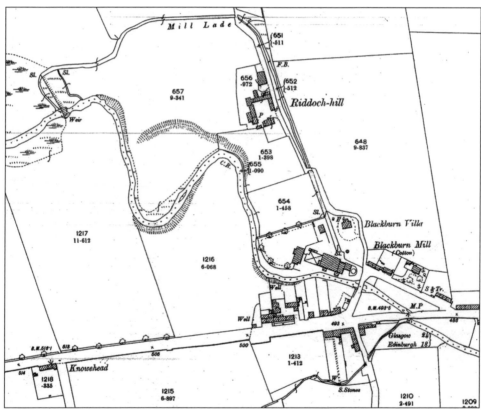

The mill lade and Cotton mill (1897)
Ordnance Survey

The Industrial Revolution, to put it simply, was the introduction of machines to do the work previously done by people, so that it could be carried out more quickly, more powerfully and more cheaply. The sources of power for the new machinery of the 18th century were water and steam. Blackburn, by the River Almond, had an abundant supply of water, and it was water that powered the Cotton Mill – the first factory to be built in the village; probably the first in the whole of West Lothian.

Spinning of wool into yarn or thread had traditionally been the work of girls and unmarried women (hence the term spinsters). Men did the weaving, and could weave in a day as much yarn as perhaps four or five spinsters could spin. So textile masters turned their attention to speeding up the spinning process to keep up with the weaving.

The spinning jenny ('jenny' was a nickname for 'engine') was invented in 1764 in Blackburn (Lancashire) by James Hargreaves; then in 1768, Richard Arkwright invented waterframe spinning, whereby cotton thread was spun on large water-powered machines, turning dozens of spindles at a time; and Samuel Crompton combined the jenny and the waterframe to produce the spinning mule in 1779. The first cotton mill in Scotland was built at Penicuik in 1778, and the second at Rothesay on the Isle of Bute in 1779. In the 1780s, David Dale opened his cotton mills at New Lanark, and other mills were built in Renfrewshire, Lanarkshire and Perthshire. There is a little-known connection between the Blackburn Cotton Mill and the New Lanark Mills, which is explained in Chapter Five. Blackburn Cotton Mill was built just 30 years after these first technological advances, so was at the forefront of an expanding industry. There were nineteen cotton mills in Scotland in 1787, and 39 by 1796, so Blackburn was one of 20 Scottish mills built in that decade.

A deed drawn up in 1794 records the feuing by William Honyman to Charles Hamilton, a Glasgow merchant, of:

> that part of my lands of Reddochhill adjoining to the Village of Blackburn... upon which a cotton mill is now erected, which is separated from my other grounds upon the east and the north by a hedge and ditch to be erected by the said Charles Hamilton, and is bounded on the west and the south by the water and Bridge of Blackburn, also the ground presently occupied by a miln head for said miln, together with the ground belonging to me and presently covered with water for a dam to said miln, and damhead.

The whole complex extended to four and a half acres, with a feu duty of £27 sterling per annum. The feu took effect from Martinmas (November) 1792. By 1794, the Cotton Mill was erected, so it seems fairly certain that it was built in 1793 by Charles Hamilton, after he took possession of the four and half acres at Riddochhill in November 1792.

Charles Hamilton

Nothing is known of Charles Hamilton, except that he was a Glasgow merchant, which may mean anything from a shop-keeper to a wealthy businessman. The latter seems more likely, since he had sufficient money to buy the land and build a mill. It is possible that he received certain incentives to come to Blackburn from William Honyman, in the hope that he would provide work for the people of the expanding village; or perhaps the good site and ample supply of water were enough to attract him. Another possible explanation is that Hamilton was just one of a number of businessmen acting in partnership, as was common with early industrial and manufacturing concerns.

Charles Hamilton raised finance for the mill operations from at least three sources. In 1796, he borrowed £1,000 from Walter Scott, the poet, novelist and Edinburgh lawyer, using his land at Riddochhill as security. With banks at an early stage of their development, it was generally individuals who lent money to commercial ventures at interest, as a means of investing their money. Another loan of £1,000 was obtained from William Honyman of Graemsay, and yet another from an unidentified source, all on the security of the Cotton Mill.

The writer of the First Statistical Account of the parish of Livingston comments that 'a water mill, to drive machinery for carding and spinning cotton, has lately been erected at the latter village [Blackburn], which, it is to be hoped, will be of use, by employing at least a part of the inhabitants.' The mill was evidently so new when he wrote in 1794 that it had not yet recruited a workforce. The village of Blackburn, the writer tells us, had 200 inhabitants, and the mill jobs were expected to attract more people to the village.

The mill was situated in the triangle of land between the Great Toll Road and Mill Road. It was a good position, close to a water supply and on a main road for bringing in supplies and sending out finished goods. The water was taken from the Almond, not immediately next to the Mill, but a hundred yards or so to the west, and was brought to the mill along a lade. There was also a millpond to help regulate the flow of water.

Blackburn was a cotton spinning mill: raw cotton wool (usually from India or the West Indies) was brought to the mill, and was carded (combed), cleaned, and spun into yarn – probably on spinning mules, comprising between 50 and 120 spindles each, turned by water power.

The size of the workforce in the early years of the mill is not known, though may have been about 30 to 50. Children would certainly have been employed as 'piecers,' for their fingers were neat and nimble enough to piece together the yarn when it snapped. It is probable that many of the workers were women, but the only names which have survived from this early period are those of men – James Cameron, a cotton carder; John Hastie and George Ferguson, cotton spinners; and James Clunes and Thomas Mathews, 'servants at the Cotton Work.'

Blackburn Cotton Mill was built at a time when even the largest industrial concerns in West Lothian, such as mines or limeworks, employed no more than about 20. It was the first factory, and the first mechanised industry, in West Lothian. It must have been a startling sight in the rural landscape: its size, the whirling spindles, the clatter of the machinery and the rush of water – the whole scale of the enterprise must have been novel and disturbing for the people of Blackburn.

Most of these houses were probably built for the cotton mill workers. The two-storey house is believed to be the 'Barracks', probably a lodging house for the accommodation of mill workers.

West Lothian Council Libraries

Assuming that the workforce was a large one for the time, the question is: where did the workers come from? There were unlikely to be sufficient people in the new village of Blackburn with its population of only some 200. The likely answer is that the workers were drawn from all over the district, and perhaps from even further afield, attracted by the regular work and relatively good wages. No apprenticeship or qualifications were needed to get a job in a cotton mill. The wages paid were considerably higher than a farm labourer could earn, so many gave up farm work and went into the mills.

If the mill attracted workers, where were they to be housed? Those seeking work were unlikely to be wealthy enough to buy their own land from George Moncrieff or William Honyman. What they required was cheap, rented accommodation. In December 1798, the Sasines record that Charles Hamilton bought some land on the Edinburgh and Glasgow Road. As Hamilton did not live in Blackburn, it seems likely that he was buying this land to house his workers. The transfer of this property was done 'in the presence of Edmund Hardie, Manager of the Blackburn Cotton Mill, and James Anderson, Cotton Spinner there...' This confirms that Charles Hamilton continued his mercantile activities in Glasgow and ran the Blackburn mill through a manager.

CHAPTER 4

Blackburn House and Estate, 1800–1845

UPON BECOMING GEORGE MONCRIEFF'S heir, Thomas Clarkson followed the custom of the time and took his name. Henceforth he was generally known as Thomas Clarkson Moncrieff. He was a professional soldier, first in the regular army, then in the fencibles, then in the militia, a temporary army enlisted for an emergency period only. By the time of his death, he was a Major in the Berwickshire Regiment of Militia, which had amalgamated with the Linlithgowshire Militia.

In addition to his army career, he had obtained a government post as Distributor of Stamps for Stirling and Clackmannan – the sort of post which involved little work, but a regular income. He owed this post to 'the interest of Mr Dundas.' Henry Dundas was the most powerful politician in Scotland. With thousands of government posts in his gift, he used them, as was customary and expected at the time, to buy votes for the government. Thomas Clarkson no doubt got his post on the tacit understanding that he would use his vote in the Tory government's favour. In addition to these two sources of income, he owned the small estate of Whitehill (formerly Wester Inch) between Bathgate and Blackburn, and was sufficiently wealthy to keep a carriage.

Because of his other interests, Thomas Clarkson had little time to devote to the management of the Blackburn estate after he inherited it in 1798. A deed survives which shows that soon after taking over, he let Easter Inch to Alexander Marjoribanks of Balbardie for a period of 38 years. Part of the lease agreement was that Alexander Marjoribanks should drain the Moss, divide it into six parks (enclosed fields) and plant six 'belts or stripes of ground running south and north,' to be planted with 'oaks, beeches and larix [larch trees] intermixed, each belt to be at least 30 feet wide.'

The terms of the lease suggest that Alexander Marjoribanks intended to use the land he reclaimed from the Moss as pasture, sheltered by wide belts of trees, but his plan to drain the moss was the first of several unsuccessful drainage schemes over the next two centuries. The Moss at that time was used only for digging peats and coal, for there is a mention in the lease of a road 'entering the Moss at the centre by the Middle Farm, being the present Peat and Coal Road.'

Thomas Clarkson Moncrieff continued to feu off land in Blackburn, though to a much lesser extent than had George Moncrieff and William Honyman. His ownership of Blackburn was brief – 1798 to 1805 – but he is the earliest owner of whom some memories survive. During the 1880s, the beginning of the 19th century was still within living memory, and the *West Lothian Courier* published a series of reminiscences. An old 'Residenter' recalled that Major Clarkson had offered to donate the 'Hill' or Knowe at the west end of Blackburn to the village, if the villagers would undertake to establish a cattle market there. The scheme, for whatever reason, failed. The Knowe, (opposite St Kentigern's Academy) was the site of the annual games which were said to have been held since 1750, at least. The old residenter also recalled that Major Clarkson and his daughter used to attend the games and 'his daughter entered into the dancing that took place on the Hill.'

Towards the end of his life, Thomas Clarkson Moncrieff's affairs were in some disorder. He sold the estate of Blackburn to Thomas Douglas in 1805, and seems to have moved to Woodbridge in Suffolk, where he died in April 1811, aged about 70. Surprisingly, he died intestate. The beneficiary was his daughter and only child, Catharine, but the surprising fact is that he left so little money: 'the said Umquhile [late] Thomas Clarkson Moncrieff had pertaining and belonging to him at the time of his death foresaid, the sum of Ten pounds, being part of the Amount of the Inventory of his Personal estate...' Any property in the form of land or houses would have been disposed of separately, and presumably it also came to his daughter Catharine.

Catharine's daughter, Catherine Moncrieff Norton, married John Sinclair of the Theatre Royal, Covent Garden, London, in 1816, and had a son named John Moncrieff Sinclair, born in Edinburgh in 1824. The line of descent of the Clarkson Moncrieffs cannot be traced any further.

Thomas Douglas

The house and estate of Blackburn were sold by Thomas Clarkson to Thomas Douglas in 1805 for £12,082. Douglas was a 'coalmaster and worker of ironstone' at Kendrieshill, Stirlingshire, and developed some small coal mines in the Blackburn area. A few years previously he had bought the estate of Easter Inch from Clarkson.

Thomas Douglas was something of an entrepreneur who bought and sold land as a commodity to raise money and finance his ventures. In the seven years between his purchase of Blackburn and his affairs having to go into administration, 66 land transactions by him are recorded in the Register of Sasines. His ventures did not always succeed, and as he struggled to bring his books into order, he broke up and sold off the Blackburn estate. Almost before his purchase of the Blackburn estate was completed, he had advertised the Middle Lot for sale again. It consisted of 274 acres, centred on the mansion house, and the advertisement in the *Edinburgh Evening Courant* described it in typical estate agents' terms:

> This beautiful and delightful property lies in the county of Linlithgow, 17 miles from Edinburgh on the Glasgow road by Whitburn. It consists of 274 acres 75 parts. The inclosures have hedge rows and belts of thriving planting. The Water of Almond, a fine trouting river, is the south boundary. On the lands, plenty of game will be found. They are of excellent soil and fit for wheat and turnip husbandry; and only require to be examined to give satisfaction.
>
> The Mansion-house is in excellent repair, from which the castle of Edinburgh and the whole intervening and adjoining country is seen. It consists of five fine apartments, besides others; the dining and drawing rooms are large and elegant. The bed-rooms are also all large, and have a dressing closet off each. There is a complete set of offices; a kitchen garden; with a lawn in front and rear of the house.
>
> If a purchaser inclines, he can also have from 40 to 60 acres on the south side of the river, and by planting the south bank thereof, the place would be rendered still more picturesque.

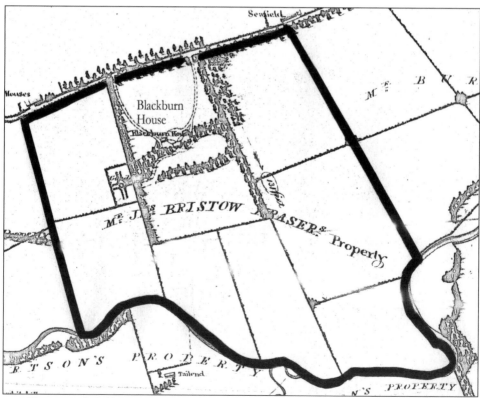

The extent of Blackburn estate after Thomas Douglas broke it up and sold off most of the land.
Ordnance Survey

The Middle Lot failed to find a buyer, but in late 1806, Thomas Douglas sold the West Lot of Blackburn estate – Torr, Toshackbrae, Whitehill and Tailend Farms, comprising 188 acres. (There were two Whitehill Farms in the Blackburn area. This Whitehill was south of the Almond; the other was the site of the present-day industrial estate.) In December of that same year, Seafield Farm was sold to John Burd of Stirling; and in 1808, Redhouse Farm and moss ground to the north of it were sold to Robert Forsyth, an advocate and the author of a five-volume work, *The Beauties of Scotland*, published in 1805–08. Forsyth lived in Edinburgh and only 'occasionally at Redhouse'. Also in 1808, the mill and mill lands of Blackburn were sold to William Callendar.

The estate of Blackburn, now reduced to less than a sixth of its size when Moncrieff acquired it, was sold for £11,000 in 1810, but it was not enough to save Thomas Douglas' affairs from being sequestered in 1812. Easter Inch estate passed eventually to Douglas' nephew, Mr Fleming of Craigs, then to John Waddell, a wealthy civil engineering contractor and a provost of Bathgate. It was he who built the fine farm steadings which have now been converted into housing as Easter Inch Grange.

After Moncrieff, Clarkson and Douglas, the owners of Blackburn House took little interest in the village of Blackburn. It was no longer an estate village, but had acquired independence from its founding patrons, George Moncrieff and William Honyman, and so the constantly changing ownership of Blackburn House hardly affected the village's progress.

James Bristow Fraser

The new owner of the shrunken Blackburn estate was James Bristow Fraser. A lawyer, he was sole trustee of the sequestered estate of Wilsontown whose huge Cleugh ironworks, among the earliest in Scotland, had run into financial difficulties. As trustee, his job was to sell the works on behalf of the creditors. Fraser's other interest was steam power for boats. In 1819 he took out a patent for 'certain improvements in the application of Machinery for propelling boats or other Vessels floating in or upon water and for attaining other useful purposes by means of an hydro pneumatic apparatus acted upon by a steam engine or other adequate power.'

With his professional work at the Cleugh ironworks, and his experiments in steam-powered vessels, Fraser had no time or inclination to farm his new estate. In 1812 he put the farmland up for public roup (auction) at the sheriff courthouse of Linlithgow. The land comprised 'six enclosures [fields] bounded by the lands of Seafield on the east, the water of Almond on the south, the land sold by Thomas

Douglas of Easter Inch to William Callendar of Renton [Foulshiels] on the west, and the Great High Road to Glasgow on the north.' These six fields were all that remained of the estate that once supported Blackburn mansion house.

The land was to be let for seventeen years and the reserve price was £260 annual rent. James Bristow Fraser undertook to build the new tenant a one-storey house with stable and byre at 'the north west corner of the Wester or Garden park immediately opposite the red houses,' but until that house was built, the tenant was to live in 'the lower part of mansion house.'

At the public roup, Alex Thornton Jr., son of the tenant of Carmondean Farm, secured the land for a rent of £264 per year. There is no evidence that the one-storey house opposite Redhouse Farm was ever built, so perhaps the mansion house was flatted at that time.

James Bristow Fraser remained the trustee of the Wilsontown ironworks until 1821, when the works and mines were sold to the great Lanarkshire coalmaster, William Dixon. James Fraser's finances were damaged by the collapse of the Stirling Banking Company and in late September 1828 his estate was sequestered and passed into the hands of trustees. In 1832, Blackburn House and its remaining 104 acres were put up for sale yet again.

William Erskine

The new owner was William Erskine, who is described as 'late of Bombay, sometime residing at Pau in France, now at Blackburn.' The purchase price was £6,800, substantially less than the £11,000 paid by Fraser in 1812. This may have been due to the depression in agriculture following the end of the Peninsular Wars in 1815; or perhaps Fraser's trustees accepted less than the true value of the estate in order to get it sold.

William Erskine was presumably one of the 'nabobs,' the merchants and officials of the East India Company who returned home to Britain with vast wealth at their disposal. They bought land, not necessarily to live on, but as an investment. Erskine and his wife lived for a time in the Chateau de Betheres near Pau in the south of France, where they had three daughters. A son, Henry, was born at Blackburn House, and baptised there in 1831 by the Episcopal Bishop of Edinburgh. Later, William Erskine let the house to an army major, Alexander Horsburgh and his family. In 1845, William Erskine sold the estate of Blackburn to Andrew Sceales, a ropemaker, of Jamaica Street in Leith. The Sceales (or Scales) family had an existing connection with Blackburn through their purchase of the Mill of Blackburn in 1823 from William Callendar's widow.

Once the estate of Blackburn had been reduced by Thomas Douglas to a rump of just 104 acres and the mansion house, it was too small to provide sufficient income for a gentleman to live on. For most of the 19th century, the income from the estate had to be supplemented from other sources – lawyers' fees, business ventures, or a private fortune. The owners of Blackburn House no longer owned the village (except as feudal superiors), so had not the paternal interest in it shown by Moncrieff and Honyman. The major influence on Blackburn's development in the nineteenth century was not agriculture in the person of the 'laird,' but industry in the shape of cotton and coal. Earlier than most communities, the people of Blackburn were freed from the power of the laird. The influence of the Church was also less than it might have been if the minister and most of the elders had been based in Blackburn rather than Livingston. But a new force replaced the power of the laird and the minister – the mill-owner and his managers.

CHAPTER 5

The Cotton Mill: William Kelly and Robert Thom

William Kelly in 1802.
Enamel medallion by
John Henning.

Paisley Museums and Art Galleries

IN 1803, CHARLES HAMILTON sold the Blackburn Cotton Mill to William Kelly, a man of some significance in the early history of the Scottish cotton industry. William Kelly was a young Lanarkshire clockmaker who was recruited by David Dale to use his gear-cutting skills on the larger machinery of the New Lanark Cotton Mills. He was an able employee and rose to become joint manager of the mills, together with David Dale's half-brother, James.

William Kelly devised several important improvements in cotton spinning technology, including a powered spinning machine. His 1792 patent is still to be seen in the Mitchell Library: 'new invented improvements in spinning machinery, by the application of which all and every kind of these spinning machines, commonly called jennies, may be spun by water, by steam, or by horses instead of manual labour only, which has been the practice hitherto, and these improvements are applicable not only to machines which may be made in future, but also those at present in use, which will be of great utility.' This was the first time that water power had been used in spinning, but Kelly's method proved unsatisfactory and was not widely adopted.

In 1793, the *Scots Magazine* recorded that 'The Honourable Board of Trustees for Fisheries, Manufactures, and Improvements in Scotland, has been pleased to award a premium to Mr William Kelly, principal manager of the cotton-works of David Dale, Esq., at Lanark, for an ingenious improvement in the method of constructing the Great Gear, or large machinery of cotton mills; which requires less water, prevents stoppages of the machinery, and saves children from accidents.' Other experiments of Kelly's led to improved heating. Cotton mills were highly susceptible to fire, so Kelly's system involved a stove and a series of hot air ducts to reduce the risk of sparks.

Kelly's Clock

The most visible reminder of his contribution to New Lanark is the huge mill clock which was made by William Kelly and which now stands at the entrance to the Visitor centre. It was described by an American visitor in 1795: 'There is a remarkable clock with a face something larger than a common clock. It has five dials, one for the hours and minutes and seconds; one for the weeks; one for the months; one for the years; one for the ten years... by which they regulate the mills, as the same wheel turns the clock and the mill.'

It is clear that David Dale thought highly of William Kelly, as the erstwhile clockmaker was promoted to manager and lived latterly in the manager's house (now called Robert Owen's house), which still stands in the centre of the village. In 1799, however, David Dale sold New Lanark to his son-in-law, Robert Owen, who had new ideas to introduce to the mills and village. In 1800, Owen sacked the two joint managers, claiming that they were 'incompetent to comprehend my views or to assist me in my plans.'

Redundant, but by no means disgraced, William Kelly moved to Glasgow and took up cotton broking. Then he moved back into cotton manufacture, and in 1803 bought the Blackburn Cotton Mill from Charles Hamilton for £3,000 sterling.

The Sasine recording the sale describes the site of the Cotton Mill: 'that part of the lands of Reddochhill adjoining to the village of Blackburn and machinery and utensils belonging thereto, together with the Cotton Mill erected thereon...' The manager of the work is named as Henry Kelly. As Kelly was not a common name in Scotland at the time, it is possible that Henry Kelly was a relative who drew William Kelly's attention to the sale of the Blackburn Cotton Mill.

There is a frustrating lack of records of Kelly's time at Blackburn. If the *West Lothian Courier* of 1877 is to be believed, a fire destroyed the Cotton Mill in 1805, and it had to be rebuilt. Perhaps Kelly had not introduced his safer heating method to Blackburn.

With his years at New Lanark still fresh in his memory, it seems likely that William Kelly attempted to introduce some of the humane and revolutionary methods of factory organisation which he had learned under David Dale. When he later took over the Rothesay Cotton Mills, he introduced New Lanark-style labour relations to Rothesay: built workers' houses and provided a company shop selling good quality goods and services. Details of his management at Blackburn are lacking, but its seems unlikely that he would have implemented these enlightened policies in New Lanark and Rothesay, but not in Blackburn during the years in between. David Dale at New Lanark had provided decent housing for his workforce, so it is probable that Kelly's purchase, on the same day as the mill, of 22 falls and nine ells of land on the north side of the main road, was to build houses for his workforce. A further '20 falls of ground and piece of ground adjacent thereto with the buildings thereon on the north side of the Edinburgh and Glasgow road' were purchased by William Kelly in 1815. David Dale provided good schooling from nursery years upwards for the New Lanark children; village tradition in Blackburn says that an early mill-owner built a school for the mill children, and one was certainly in existence by 1855.

It's certain that William Kelly, one of the pioneers of water power in spinning, used the waters of the Almond to power Blackburn Cotton Mill. Probably, however, Kelly retained his Glasgow interests and managed Blackburn Mill through a manager. Henry Kelly may have continued for a while, but within a year or two a new manager was in place, one of the most prominent men to be associated with the village: Robert Thom.

Robert Thom

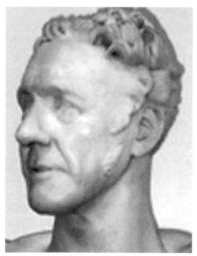

Robert Thom.
Sculpture by Patric Park, 1835.
McLean Museum and Art Gallery,
Inverclyde Council

Robert Thom was born in Tarbolton, Ayrshire in 1774 and in his youth worked on his father's farm. Apprenticed to an older brother, he became a wright (joiner) and moved to Glasgow. There he continued his education at University evening classes and was offered the post of manager of the Pollockshaws Cotton Mills. From Pollockshaws, he moved to Blackburn, and was certainly there by 1808, when he was 34 years of age. At some date before August of that year, William Kelly had raised capital by forming the Blackburn Spinning Company, and Robert Thom was invited to become its managing partner.

The Company's earliest recorded act was to buy 'a portion of land and houses thereon' at Blackburn. As they were being sold by Thomas Mair of Pottishaw, it may be assumed they were at the west end of the village, and that they were to accommodate more mill workers.

In 1813, Robert Thom 'partner and manager of the Blackburn Spinning Company' bought a 'portion of ground with the houses thereon on the north side of the great toll road' at the east end of the village. And in 1815, Kelly purchased 20 falls of land 'with the buildings thereon' on the north side of the Edinburgh-Glasgow road. The number of houses owned by the Company at this time is not known but the regular purchase of property suggests a constantly expanding workforce.

Robert Thom's particular interest was water supply: he was unimpressed by steam power and was later to become Scotland's foremost civil engineer for water supply. 'Get water power if you can,' he wrote, 'and be quit of these smoky and expensive engines.'

'Mr Thom was in the belief that, with his sluices and water cuts, he would retain mills and workers in country districts, driven by water instead of steam... One great reason Mr Thom gave for his fondness of country workers was their superiority of character.' Strange then, that in 1809 the following case should have come before the Kirk Session of Livingston:

> Mr Robert Tom [sic] having compeared voluntarily before the Session for the sin of fornication was rebuked and suitably admonished. He was absolved from the scandal. He presented the Session with Three Guineas for the behoof the poor as a token of his contrition.

And in 1814, when Thom was forty and about to marry a seventeen year old girl:

> Compeared before them Mary Aitkin acknowledging Robert Thom Esq. of Blackburn, the father of a female child born by her about three years ago, the moderator produced the following letter from Mr Thom acknowledging his guilt:
> 'Sir,
> Mary Aitkin has called upon me for a line acknowledging that I am the father of her child, which is a question which she alone can answer – but I admit having had connection with her about that time.
> I am, Sir, Your Most Obed^t Servant,
> Rt Thom,
> Blackburn, July 16th, 1814'
> The Session fined the parties in three guineas for the poor of the parish.

It seems that Robert Thom required 'superiority of character' only in the work-force and not in the management. Two other men connected with the Cotton Mill appeared before the Kirk Session on similar charges: William Houstoun, manager of the Blackburn Cotton Mill, admitted fornication with Margaret Boag, and 'as a mark of penitence after being suitably admonished by the Moderator, gave £1 1s for the benefit of the poor of the parish.'

And in 1822: 'Ann Wilson residing in Blackburn appeared [before the Session] declaring that she had brought forth a child in fornication and declared Alex. Brown of the Cotton Mill in Blackburn as the father of her child.' The Session ordered him to appear before them, but instead he wrote admitting the charge, which suggests he was a manager rather than an ordinary worker.

In these cases we see the Church taking what seems to modern eyes a prurient interest in the private lives of ordinary people. In fact the Session played a useful role in these cases. Robert Thom was the most powerful man in Blackburn, and Mary Aitkin had clearly been unable to get him to acknowledge the child or contribute to its support. It's possible that she voluntarily approached the Session knowing that they could put pressure on Thom to acknowledge paternity. In effect the Session was acting as an early form of Child Support Agency.

In 1813, William Kelly and Robert Thom purchased the Rothesay Cotton Mill. It was the second earliest cotton mill in Scotland, having been established in 1779. It was a large concern, but nevertheless went bankrupt in 1812, so Kelly and Thom were able to acquire it cheaply.

We know from the letter concerning Mary Aitkin that Robert Thom was still resident in Blackburn in 1814, but certainly by 1817 he and Kelly had moved to Rothesay. Thereafter they ran the Blackburn Mill through managers such as the Walter Houstoun fined for fornication in 1816. Houstoun continued as manager for several years and was also a partner in the Blackburn Spinning Company. His

Robert Thom's gravestone,
Rothesay Churchyard

Brian Cavanagh

fellow partners were John Houstoun, a Glasgow manufacturer and probably a relative; Robert Thom; and John Dougal, a Rothesay cotton spinner.

In 1825, William Kelly and his son William sold their share of Blackburn Cotton Mill to Robert Thom and the Blackburn Spinning Company, and in 1825–6 sold Rothesay Cotton Mill to their partner, Robert Thom, for £24,900. William Kelly retired from business life, and died in 1846.

By 1834, Thom had disposed of his remaining interest in the Blackburn Cotton Mill and was gaining distinction as a civil engineer. One of the problems of Rothesay's previous owners had been a shortage of water, which had forced the owner to introduce two steam engines. To remedy the water shortage, Thom built a series of drains over six miles in length, with self-acting sluices to collect a supply of water into Loch Fad. This water kept the works operational even in a dry season, and the steam engines were abandoned. The success of these measures encouraged him to further study of hydraulic civil engineering, and he was invited to work on the Greenock water supply. There he managed to combine the supply of water power for machinery with a public water supply. The reservoir he created in the hills above the town was named Loch Thom in his honour, and a walk with fine views over Greenock and the Firth of Clyde has been created around his 'cuts.'

Thom undertook or advised on the building of other public water supplies. In 1840, by now a wealthy man, he retired from business to his estate of Ascog just south of Rothesay, where he died in 1847. He was writing a book *On the Supply of Water to Towns* at the time of his death.

CHAPTER 6

The Other Blackburn Mills

BLACKBURN COTTON MILL WAS not the only industrial venture in early 19th century Blackburn. Every agricultural estate had its own mill, which was generally a source of income to the estate, as all the tenants were 'thirled' to the estate's mill: that is, they were obliged to use the estate mill for the grinding of their corn. With a captive clientele, the miller, if he was unscrupulous, could charge what he wanted, skimp on the work and help himself to the tenants' grain. Not all millers were dishonest, but they were often unpopular figures.

Mills always had some land attached to them for the millers' livestock or crops; these were known as the mill lands. The corn mills of the 18th century were water-powered. If a river did not provide sufficient force or a regular enough supply, a mill lade would be led off the river upstream, bringing the water to a small reservoir, the millpond or dam. The Mill of Blackburn lade came off the River Almond at the Haugh. The lade flowed underneath the mill buildings (powering the indoor mill wheel), then flowed on eastwards to bring water to Hopefield Mill on the Wester Breich road. A shared lade was possible as for many years the two mills were run as a joint venture.

The Mill of Blackburn was a substantial complex of buildings south of East Main Street. It lay just east of the present civic amenity site, under what are now Matt Purdie's warehouses. The mill was built in the form of two L-shaped buildings round a courtyard. Until the early 19th century the mill formed part of the Blackburn Estate. In 1808, as part of his 'asset stripping,' Thomas Douglas sold the Mill of Blackburn, together with the mill lands, dam and lade, to William Callendar, an Edinburgh lawyer.

A lawyer was not going to take to corn milling; he had another plan for the mill. He converted it to a distillery and it continued for many years afterwards to be referred to as the Stell (or still). It was not a good time for such a venture: customs duties on spirits were high and constantly being raised still higher. A great many distilleries were in fact closing down at this period because of the crippling taxes and the resultant prevalence of smuggled whisky. By 1813, there were only 24 (legal) distillers in the whole of Scotland and the duty stood at 9s 4¼d a gallon. The ill-timed distillery venture was short-lived, and Callendar let his mill buildings briefly to a wool-spinning firm.

By 1823, Callendar was dead, and his widow put the Mill of Blackburn up for sale, together with the third mill in Blackburn – Hopefield Mill on the River Almond, by the bridge on the Wester Breich Road.

When Hopefield Mill was built, or by whom, is not known. It is probable that it was built as a corn mill in the 18th century, then turned into a paper mill at some date between 1800 and 1817. The waters of the River Almond, brought to the mill by the Mill of Blackburn lade, were used to mix beaten rags of linen or cotton into a liquid pulp, which was then laid on wire moulds, pressed, sized with animal glue, pressed again till smooth, then dried and cut. The paper mill was a small operation with just one vat, and its establishment was probably influenced by the presence of the Cotton Mill nearby, which ensured a ready supply of cotton waste.

Forgery

In 1817, William Clark, paper maker at Blackburn Paper Mill, was imprisoned in the Tolbooth of Edinburgh, accused of forging official stamps on his paper (to avoid paying tax). The charge was dismissed on a technicality. His son, John Clark, 'lately residing in the village of Blackburn,' was accused of the same crime; when he failed to appear for trial, he was declared an outlaw and fugitive from His Majesty's laws.

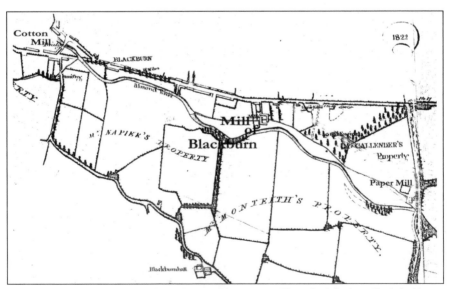

Blackburn in 1822. All three mills can be seen: the Cotton Mill on the left, the Mill of Blackburn, and Hopefield Paper Mill. The shared mill lade to the Mill of Blackburn and Hopefield Mill runs north of the Almond.

National Archives of Scotland, RHP 3599

When the two mills, Blackburn and Hopefield, were put up for sale in 1823, they were purchased by James Sceales. He was a Leith rope and sailcloth manufacturer, part of a large and well-to-do family business. For a time, Sceales continued to lease Hopefield Mill to the paper manufacturer Adam Manson & Co., but in the late 1820s he took Hopefield Mill back into his own hands, and converted it to a flax spinning mill. In 1823, the law requiring official stamping of linen had been abolished, thus reducing the cost of linen manufacture, and this may have been what encouraged James Sceales to buy and convert the mills.

At the Hopefield flax spinning mill, the flax (probably imported from Ireland) was spun into coarse linen thread. Sceales converted the Mill of Blackburn into a canvas weaving workshop, to which the linen thread was taken to be woven on looms into canvas. An elderly Blackburn woman recalled growing up among the miners of Bo'ness in the 1840s and 1850s: 'it was from Blackburn that most of the cloth was obtained at Bo'ness to make the aprons, gowns, and other garments – good, hard wearing material that seemed never to go done.' Old Councillor Ross in 1908 recalled that Blackburn canvas was used mainly for ship sails and awnings. Also in 1908, a Miss White of Blackburn still possessed a piece of the canvas woven in Blackburn Mill. 'It is of strong material, and has the appearance of being newly manufactured, so fresh and of good quality is the material with which it must have been made.'

At the Hopefield Mill, the fibres of flax would have been beaten, then 'heckled' (straightened and combed). Next, the yarn was spun, bleached, and if required, dyed. At the Mill of Blackburn, the linen thread was woven into canvas, which was then rubbed, cropped of loose fibres and given a smooth surface by calendering (being passed between heavy rollers). Flax spinning and weaving were difficult to mechanise. Flax contains a gum, so its fibres become sticky. Hand workers dealt with this by separating the glued fibres, but machines tended to get gummed up, or to break the gummed fibres. Hand looms rather than steam looms prevailed until these problems were resolved about 1840. From then on the industry became concentrated in large mechanised factories in the east, particularly in the huge jute mills of Dundee.

Flax spinning was an unpleasant and unhealthy occupation. According to the factory inspector's report of 1848:

from the innumerable particles of the dust and fibre of the raw material with which the air of these factories is loaded, it is extremely disagreeable to remain in one of these rooms, even for ten minutes; for you cannot do so without experiencing a sensation of considerable distress, in consequence of the eyes, ears, nostrils and mouth being filled with the clouds of flax dust from which there is no escape on any side.

By 1830, the flax spinning mill at Hopefield employed some 46 people. Most of them were young. In 1836, the factory inspector listed their ages.

Age	Number of Employees	Age	Number of Employees
9	4	16	4
10	4	17	3
11	6	18	2
12	9	19	2
13	5	20	0
14	4	over 20	3
15	0		

So, of 46 workers, 32 were under the age of 16, and only three were over 21. Two thirds were female. Spinning was fiddly work; when the threads broke, nimble fingers were required to mend them, so children and young women were preferred for the work; and of course, they could be paid much less than a man.

Together the flax spinning mill at Hopefield and the sailcloth manufactory at the Mill of Blackburn employed nearly 200 people. Some 50 looms were employed in weaving the canvas cloth. All were water-powered, as in the 1830s steam power had not yet come to Blackburn.

Also at Hopefield was a thread-dyeing department. In 1886, a *West Lothian Courier* writer met an old man called Archie Dunlop:

Half a century ago, Archie had charge of the dyeing department in Sceales' flax mill here, and a fine specimen of his skill is stowed away in the 'shottle of the kist,' in the shape of a bunch of linen threads, with 24 different colours, and shades of colours, every colour showing as clear and distinct as when they were dyed 50 years ago.

The contemporary word for canvas was 'duck,' or in Scots, 'dook.' The cottages which housed some of the canvas workers were known as Dook Raw, and the buildings and the name survived into the 20th century. Dook Raw stood on the south side of East Main Street, a little to the east of the former Picturedrome. It was a row at right angles to the Main Street and consisted of at least five houses occupied until the 1930s. Reminiscences in the *West Lothian Courier* in 1908 claimed that the flax dressers of the Dook Raw used to club together to buy a *Scotsman* newspaper, which was read by each in turn. The last one to get it was allowed to keep it. Presumably these newspaper readers were the adult male flax weavers, not the teenage and child workers of the flax spinning mill.

Despite employing the cheap labour of women and children, James Sceales was unable to make a success of the business. In 1840, his firm was sequestrated and the flax spinning mill and canvas factory closed down. Many of the unemployed left the village to seek work elsewhere. The decline in population (from 422 persons in 1831, to 391 in 1841) was noted by the census enumerator: 'The decrease of 31 may be accounted for by the stoppage of the Flax Mill and sail-cloth manu-factory which employed nearly 200 hands.' The loss of so large a concern was a serious matter. Together the two mills had employed more than twice the number employed at the Cotton Mill.

According to a much later article in the *West Lothian Courier*, James Sceales' manager, William Neil (who lived in Hopefield Cottage, across the Breich road from Redhouse School), reopened the canvas weaving factory in the Mill of Blackburn and carried it on till his death. Then his older son, Henry, though still just a teenager, took it over, but by the mid 1840s, had to give up, 'being unable to compete with the steam loom.' Thus water power was ousted from Blackburn mid-century by the power of steam.

James Sceales died about this time, for in late 1846, it was not he but his trustees who accepted an offer for the Mill of Blackburn (the former distillery and canvas weaving mill). The new owner was John Sayer, miller at Bathgate Corn Mill. The complex of mill buildings was converted into dwelling houses. By 1877, they were described as old and dilapidated, and by 1895, had been demolished, and today are wholly forgotten. Only Dook Raw remains within the memory of the oldest inhabitants. The course of the mill lade can be traced in the waste ground along the riverside. Hopefield Mill's later history is traced in Chapter Eight.

Sceales' flax spinning mill and sailcloth factory preceded any other factory in West Lothian – except, of course, Blackburn Cotton Mill and the early cotton manufactory in Whitburn, which employed only 30–40; and it far exceeded both these cotton mills in numbers of employees. It was a larger employer than any of the coal mines of the time, and it predates the Bathgate Chemical Works, and the shale oil industry. Blackburn, with its three textile mills, was the first community in West Lothian to be industrialised.

CHAPTER 7

The Cotton Mill, 1830–1877

Working in the Mill

IT WAS COTTON WHICH inaugurated the factory system: demand for it outstripped supply, so the manufacturers looked for ways to increase production. It was the first manufacture in the world to be industrialised.

No matter how humane the master, working conditions in cotton factories at the beginning of the 19th century were very hard. The yarn had to be kept warm and damp to prevent its breaking, so that conditions were often unbearably hot and wet. The working day was ten or twelve hours long and discipline was strict. To workers who had been used to setting their own pace in fields or small work-shops, the transition to the grinding discipline of a factory must have been strange and unsettling. Hours were long and the atmosphere was unhealthy. Yet there was no shortage of recruits; after all, farm workers worked long hours in all weathers for meagre pay. Cotton mills at least offered regular wages, and steady work.

In the mid 1830s, the government introduced factory inspectors whose job it was to enforce the health and safety legislation which was beginning to regulate child labour and safety in factories and mills. The first legislation was the Factory Act of 1819, by which no children under the age of nine were to be employed in cotton mills. Children aged between nine and twelve could be employed for no more than nine hours a day or 48 hours a week. This legislation was much needed because so many young children were employed in the cotton industry. Later legislation further reduced children's hours of work and they became known as half-timers: they were allowed to work only part of a day and had to spend at least two hours in school.

Mrs Stein, born Mary Fisher in Blackburn in 1835. As a young girl she went as a 'half-timer' to Blackburn Cotton Mills.

West Lothian Courier
8 June 1928

The 1833 Factory Act introduced two full days' holiday a year – Christmas Day and Good Friday – and eight half-day holidays in the course of the year. Generous conditions indeed! In 1847, the maximum number of working hours in a day was set at eleven hours for adult females; then in 1848, the famous Ten Hours Act further limited the working day for all adults. There was some opposition from the workforce, who were paid hourly and thus saw their earning power being eroded. But since a Saturday half-day holiday was not general until the 1870s and 1880s, the average working week for adults in the Cotton Mill was still sixty hours. (Sunday was never a working day.)

In 1836, 100 people were employed in the Blackburn Cotton Mill. As the Scottish average at that time was 180, Blackburn can be considered a small mill. Of the 100, 45 were male and 55 were female. Until the spinning mules were mechanised, great strength was required to turn the driving wheel, so spinners were always men. The mules might weigh some 1,600 lbs and be moved the equivalent of twenty miles every day. The work was so strenuous that few spinners survived in the job beyond the age of 40. Each spinner required at least three piecers (to piece together the threads when they broke), so a high proportion of a cotton mill labour force was always children and young women – whose wages were less than half those of an adult male. Six of the Blackburn workers were just nine years old and only 32 were over 21, so two thirds were children or young people. In 1839 the figures were very similar: of 100 employees, 60 were under 21, and only 40 were over 21.

By 1846, there were 114 employed (56 males and 58 females), but 62 were eighteen or under; sixteen were children under the age of thirteen. By 1850, the proportion of young people had increased still further; 88 of the 118 employees were teenagers. No women over the age of eighteen were employed; all the adult workers (30 of them) were men. The conclusion is depressing but inescapable: like the flax works, Blackburn Cotton Mill was a child-powered industry.

For these young people, it was most certainly an unhealthy industry. Hard work at too early an age, poor diet, and lack of light and fresh air stunted growth. The average height of seventeen to eighteen year old male mill workers in 1836 was a mere five feet. Today, they would be some nine to eleven inches taller.

Against the disadvantages of hard work, long hours, unpleasant and unhealthy conditions, has to be set the fact that at first, an adult cotton mill worker was well paid, compared with an agricultural servant or general labourer. A male cotton worker might earn up to £1 a week in the good times around 1800. These high rates of pay, however, brought an influx of workers, which tended to depress wages. The first trade unions were groups of workers trying to protect their wages by limiting recruitment to the industry; in other words, protective practices were sought by the workers themselves. When wages fell at the end of the Peninsular Wars (1815), a series of strikes took place in West of Scotland cotton mills, but concerted action by workers was seen by the employers as illegal and unethical and was ruthlessly suppressed.

By the 1820s, the end of wartime demand and growing competition from the much larger Lancashire cotton industry was producing difficult conditions in the Scottish cotton mills. Trade unions gradually changed their role from protecting workers against incomers, to protecting workers from exploitation by the capitalist class of owners and employers.

Whether Blackburn Cotton Mill experienced the industrial unrest of the 1820s and 1830s is not known. If it did, the workers had good reason. With the introduction of steam, conditions in cotton mills were increasingly unpleasant. A temperature of between 80° and 100° Fahrenheit was usual in a steam-powered cotton mill, and the atmosphere was smelly, noisy and full of cotton dust.

Accidents

Accidents were frequent in early cotton mills, partly because of unfamiliarity with fast-moving machines. There was no legislation to force the employers to fit guards on moving parts, and many of the youthful workers were probably heedless of danger. The Factory Inspectors' reports of accidents make horrifying reading. Most accidents were caused by clothing, hair or hands getting caught in moving machinery. Sometimes limbs were torn off. In the worst cases the victim was trapped in the machinery, and whirled round a shaft revolving at 120 times a minute, beating the poor victim to pulp against the ceiling. Only a gradual process of accident reporting, followed by legislation, eventually reduced the dangers in the working environment.

The Cotton Spinning Process

The raw cotton was imported from North America, India, or less frequently Egypt, and was brought to Blackburn Cotton Mill in large bales. The bales were opened, and the cotton was cleaned of dirt and impurities. Then the fibres were spread and beaten to disentangle the filaments and lay them parallel. The fibres were then fed into the carding machines which formed them into a frail, loose ribbon, which was pulled and straightened. The resulting lengths of cotton were fed into the spinning frames, which stretched and twisted them into cotton yarn.

At this stage the yarn was packed and sent away to be woven into cotton cloth by hand loom weavers, of whom there were many hundreds in West Lothian until about 1850; or by steam-driven weaving looms in the new factories of the West of Scotland.

The changeover from water power to steam power in Blackburn Cotton Mill happened in the late 1830s and 1840s – after Robert Thom ceased to be in charge. In 1836, the spindles were all powered by water; in 1839, eighteen sets of spindles were still driven by water, but another sixteen sets were steam-driven. By 1850, the changeover was almost complete. Of the 15,399 spindles, 52 sets were steam powered, and only sixteen still driven by water power.

Blackburn was fortunate in being able to convert easily from water to steam. Plentiful supplies of coal were available in the local area. Some less fortunate rural mills were far from any coal seams, and the transport costs of coal made them uncompetitive.

After Kelly and Thom – Gilkison & Co.

When Robert Thom sold his share in the Blackburn Spinning Company, the remaining partners were James Weir, a Bathgate surgeon, and John Steel of Summerside. The manager was James Smith, a young man in his twenties. James Weir, the surgeon, died in the early 1840s, and in 1844, the surviving company partners, James Weir junior and Andrew Mungle, sold the Mill to a Glasgow firm, Ferguson and Co. Ltd.. Their ownership was brief, for in 1852 Robert Gilkison & Co., Glasgow cotton spinners and power loom cloth manufacturers, bought land and houses from Andrew Mungle; and the following year, they bought the Cotton Mill itself, as well as the manager's house, 41 other houses and the company shop. The *Falkirk Herald* reported the purchase of the mill and 'a considerable portion of the village' (the mill workers' houses), naming the price as £7,000. The firm was said to be thinking of 'making considerable additions to the mill, and of lighting the village with gas.'

The Ettrick Shepherd's Daughter

In June 1855, the mill workers got a day's holiday when Robert Gilkison married Harriet Sidney Hogg, a daughter of James Hogg, the Ettrick Shepherd, poet and author of *Confessions of a Justified Sinner*. Hogg's widow and family had moved to Linlithgow after his death, and it was there that the couple were married. At first Gilkison and his wife lived in the mill manager's house, but within two or three years he had put in a resident manager, Hugh Hendry. At about this time, the Cotton Mill is described as 'An extensive spinning mill, with offices, gasometer, and residence of manager all in good repair. It affords employment to about 100 males and about the same number of females.'

The 1850s were not an easy decade for the cotton industry. Textile industries were always at the mercy of changes in fashion, and in the 1850s the embroidered muslin trade collapsed. Foreign imports were competing with Scottish cotton at the coarser end of the market, while the Lancashire mills provided fierce competition at the finer end. However, Gilkison & Co. persevered in Blackburn for 25 years. The workforce reached about 200 in 1856 – its highest level – and the number of spindles in the mill reached almost 20,000 in the early 1860s. But business collapsed when the American Civil War (1861–65) brought a 'cotton famine.' The Lancashire mill workers, who had no alternative sources of employment, were reduced almost to destitution, and only a nationwide appeal fund saved them from starvation. Fortunately for the Blackburn workers, other employment was available in surrounding towns, but the workforce dropped by about a third.

However, Gilkison & Co. weathered these difficult times. By 1877, the Cotton Mill had been in operation for over 80 years. Nobody in Blackburn would have been able to remember a time when it wasn't there.

The Fire

At the beginning of 1877, Blackburn Cotton Mill was still the largest employer in the village, and produced 23 tons of gray cotton every week. It employed 120, of whom about 90 were women and girls. The firm owned 36 company houses – 20 per cent of all the households in the village.

The only known photograph of Blackburn Cotton Mill was taken when the building was disused and in ruins. The tall chimney was built when steam power replaced water power.
West Lothian District Libraries

But on 21 January 1877, in the darkness of a winter morning, Blackburn Cotton Mill burned down:

The large cotton mill in the village of Blackburn, near Bathgate, belonging to Messrs Gilkison & Co., Glasgow, was totally destroyed by fire early on Saturday morning, but fortunately the occurrence was not attended by personal injury or loss of life. The mill, which was situated on the banks of the Almond, at the west end of the village, consisted of a main building, running east and west, which was 140 feet in length, 30 feet in width, and four storeys high, and a large wing on the south west side of the same height; while at the west end was the picking house, and a fireproof store, and at the east end the engine-house, with mechanics' shops above, adjoining which again was a small gas holder for supplying the premises with gas. The mill was a very old established concern, and has existed in the village from a very early date, the oldest portion of the building now burned having taken the place of a small mill which was destroyed in a similar way in 1805. From that time several important additions have been made to the building at various periods, the latest being the south west wing already alluded to, so that previous to Saturday it contained no fewer than 20,000 spindles, and gave employment to 120 persons, about three-fourths of whom were females ... The first and second storeys of the wing were occupied by the warehouse; and here on the second floor was the entrance to the whole mill, which was approached by a flight of stone steps protected by an iron railing.

It was just as the machinery was about to be set in motion on Saturday morning that the fire took place. With so much combustible material lying about, the lighting up of the building in the winter mornings and evening required to be conducted with the greatest care, and every reasonable precaution was, we believe, taken by the manager (Mr Crawford) against the risk of fire from the carrying of naked lights about the place. A species of safety lamp was accordingly used, these being lighted in the warehouse and given to certain of the older 'hands,' who were responsible for the lighting of the gas on each floor, and each night after the lights were extinguished, the manager and spinning master went through the building to ascertain if all was right. About ten minutes to six, when the workers were nearly all assembled in the mill, one of the men, named James Robertson was making the round of the second floor, lamp in hand, engaged in lighting the gas, when, having removed the cover from his lamp to trim it, a spark, or piece of the wick, fell among some of the loose cotton waste, which immediately became ignited, and those on that flat were alarmed to see a long tongue of flame shooting across one of the spinning frames, which, while they looked, became all ablaze. The dreadful cry of 'Fire' was raised, and the terrified women, who, however, seem to have behaved with a wonderful amount of courage ... came trooping from all parts of the building, and made a hasty exit. It was well that they did so, for had they lingered by a few minutes more, a tragedy ... might have been the result. On each flat a number of buckets of water are always kept in readiness for such an emergency, and with these a few of the men made a gallant fight with the fire in the hope of checking its progress, but they were soon compelled to beat a retreat by the smoke and flames which now advanced with overwhelming rapidity.

The books having been safely got out of the warehouse, Mr Crawford next proceeded to the picking house, where a quantity of cotton was in process of being cleaned. This part of the building is fireproof and is separated from the main building by iron doors. Here a large quantity of cotton was saved, and the doors being shut and damped below with ashes, prevented the fire from spreading in this direction, although one of the doors actually became red hot.

When the men got out and assembled on a rising knoll overlooking the north side of the mill, it was seen that the building was doomed. Fanned by the wind, which was blowing pretty strongly from the north west, great billows of flame, before which everything fell prostrate, surged from end to end of the mill, while their fiery spray, dashed in a thousand directions, aided the destructive work. In something less than twenty minutes the whole interior was burning like a puddler's furnace, the roar of the flames as they leaped from one flat to another striking terror into the hearts of the villagers, who were by this time nearly all on the bridge which there spans the river, looking with dismay upon the havoc the fire was making in the mill, on which many of their number were wholly dependent for their daily bread.

A small fire engine was kept on the premises but it would have been ridiculous to have attempted doing anything in the way of combating the flames with the weak squirt of water which it was capable of throwing. Other fire engines are kept at Addiewell Works, some two miles distant, but such was the rapidity of the con-flagration that it was not thought necessary to send for them.

Nevertheless, the workers were not idle. By their exertions, not a few bales of yarn were got out of the warehouse before the heat and smoke warned them to desist. Their efforts were afterwards directed to the detached stores at the west of the building, and over these, buckets of water, which both males and females assisted in filling at the adjoining lade, were freely poured. While this was going on, the south wing had caught and now the whole mill burned fiercely. Flat after flat, unable to sustain the weight of the machinery, fell in with a crashing noise; and it was only half-an-hour after the fire broke out that the roof of the main building gave way, carrying with it nearly half of the top storey walls. The heat at this time was most intense. The solidly built walls split in different places, the outer facing of sand-stone of which they were composed, peeling off in all directions, while at a distance of twenty or thirty feet, several palings in a neighbouring garden were burned.

In little over an hour and a half, the fire had completely wrecked the building. Not a stick was left standing from one end to the other in any of the four storeys – even the heavy wooden beams on which the flooring was carried were wholly consumed, and when at length the fire burned itself out, nothing remained but the bare and ruined walls, within which lay confused heaps of machinery twisted and bent into most fantastic shapes, along with stones and other rubbish. The walls of the south wing did not suffer so severely as those of the main building, which will all have to be taken down should it be decided to rebuild the mill again. The mechanics' shop at the east end was likewise destroyed, but the engine-house underneath was untouched. A large waterwheel, which supplied part of the motive-power to the mill, also remained uninjured, as did the stores at the other end.

The damage, which we believe is covered by insurance in several London offices, cannot be less than £25,000. To many of the workers, however, the burning of the mill will be an almost irreparable loss. In a small village, the removal of one of its chief industries so suddenly must entail a great amount of hardship on many families who were wholly dependent for support upon the wages which they earned in the mill, and as the building could not be replaced in less than a year or eighteen months, many who have lived in the village all their lives, will, it is feared, have to go elsewhere for employment. In the course of the week, the ruined mill was visited by large numbers of persons from all parts of the surrounding district.

The 1877 fire brought an end to Blackburn's era as a textile village. Gilkison & Co. decided not to repair and reopen the cotton mill, perhaps because by the 1870s Blackburn was an anomaly: a rural outpost of the Scottish cotton spinning industry which was increasingly concentrated in Glasgow and the West of Scotland. Small or inefficient mills were finding it hard to survive against increasing competition from both home and abroad.

Nearly 100 of the 120 mill workers lived in Blackburn, so on the face of it, the loss of the mill seems devastating. But in fact, of the 96, only seventeen were heads of households, while the other 79 were dependents – unmarried sons (9) and daughters (70) still living at home. For a household like that of Catherine Liddle, a widow with two daughters, all employed at the mill, the consequences of the fire must have been very difficult. However, the typical cotton mill worker was between thirteen and 25 (average age sixteen), and worked at the mill until she married. Her wages were a contribution to the household economy, but not the mainstay. Nevertheless, over the next four years, the population of Blackburn dropped by over 100, and 96 wage packets were lost to the town's shops and tradesmen: Blackburn's worst economic difficulty since the closure of the flax mill. To relieve the hardship, Livingston Kirk Session gave 'a boll of meal to the deserving poor, chiefly those in the west end of the parish.'

There was no shortage of jobs for the men made redundant by the loss of the mill: they would have been quickly absorbed into the local mines, oil works and chemical works in the area. It may well have been the lack of alternative work for females which drove so many families away. The 1881 Census shows a huge rise in the number of Blackburn women declaring themselves to be domestic servants or housekeepers. These were the mill-girls who had been unable to get alternative work since the mill burned down, four years earlier.

It was the end of an era; no more would Blackburn be 'the mill village, with its scores of lasses hurrying about, with white tufts in their hair, as if they had come from the North Pole.'

CHAPTER 8

After the Fire: the end of the mills

Hopefield Mill

HOPEFIELD MILL (on the Wester Breich road) had closed down as a flax spinning mill in 1840, and was sold in 1846 to John Sayer of Bathgate Mill. He converted it back into a corn mill, and lived at Hopefield Cottage. In the early 1850s, Hopefield Mill is described as 'extensive corn and flour mills... the buildings are three storeys in height, in good repair, and fitted up with three sets of grinding stones which are worked by water power.'

After John Sayer's death in 1864, his widow Ann and son William inherited Hopefield Mill as well as the Mill of Blackburn and 'other houses on the land' – presumably Dook Raw, the former cottages of the flax workers. In 1868, while still in the Sayers' ownership, Hopefield corn mill was converted back into a paper mill, under the management of John Turner. The Sayers were also diversifying into another line of business: the Crown Inn in Blackburn had been acquired.

Despite several changes of tenant, Hopefield operated as a paper mill for many years. In 1874, it was leased by James Kennedy Martin, a landowner in Torphichen parish who lived at Bridgehouse Castle. A few years later, he spotted a new opportunity.

After the fire at the Cotton Mill, part of the building was patched up and made useable again. The water wheel was undamaged, and mill machinery could be adapted for many different types of work, as shown at Hopefield Mill. J.K. Martin bought the former Cotton Mill in 1880 and started papermaking there. His lease of the original Hopefield Mill was given up in 1882. It then stood empty for several years until bought by the McKill family, better known for their various business interests in Bathgate. The mill, however, remained silent, until by 1887 it was almost ruinous.

In 1894 however, Hopefield Mill was brought back into use by the Almond Leather Board Company. (Millboard and leatherboard are types of coarse cardboard used in book-binding.) The Almond Company was a short-lived venture by John Aitken of Springfield, Linlithgow. After another change of owner, the mill was acquired in 1898 by a firm called Guild, Richardson and Company. A year later, a financial scandal was reported in the local newspaper:

> Mr G.G. Guild, managing partner of the firm of Messrs Guild, Richardson & Coy., Hopefield Paper Mill ... has without any notice to Mr Richardson, the only other partner, left the business, and his whereabouts are at present unknown. The books have been found to be in confusion...

The firm's affairs could not be righted, so once again the mill was sold, this time to a Glasgow papermaker, A. Anderson. This and several other ventures were also short-lived. Presumably this is the mill referred to in a brief *West Lothian Courier* report in April 1901: 'James Taylor, foreman in the Hopefield Flock Mill, Blackburn, fractured his arm when his hand caught in the belt of one of the machines.' Flock is powdered wool or cotton, used to make flock wallpaper or cheap flock mattresses. But the small, rural paper mill was no longer viable, because paper-making was becoming a large-scale industry, concentrated in factories which could achieve cost savings by the huge scale of their operations. The last papermakers moved out about 1904, and by 1907 the mill was in ruins. The mill lade can still be seen as it crosses the field towards the mill, but all that remains today of Hopefield Mill is a cluster of grassy hummocks and the fragments of a retaining wall by the River Almond, at the north west corner of the bridge on the Wester Breich road.

Revival and Ruin

After the fire, the Cotton Mill buildings were sold by Gilkison & Co. to a Glasgow man called T.R. Johnston, who promptly sold them on to J.K. Martin of Hopefield Paper Mill. As has already been noted, he set up the Hopefield Millboard Company in part of the former Cotton Mill and operated it from 1880. For a time his mill manager was William Gardner, whose wife, Agnes Dunlop, had begun work at the Cotton Mill as a girl of just eight years of age. When the mill reopened as a paper mill after the fire, she had found work there, and married William Gardner, a fellow worker. In her later years she was popularly known in Blackburn as Granny, and died aged 82 as late as 1937.

J.K. Martin died in the early 1890s, but his company carried on paper making until about 1897. The mill then lay unused until 1900, when the site was bought by William Honyman of Torbanehill. Thus after 106 years, the mill site returned to the ownership of the family which had sold it to Charles Hamilton back in 1792. By the autumn of 1901 the mill was in ruins. After over 80 years of cotton spinning and some 20 years of paper-making, the story of Blackburn Cotton Mill came to an end.

Little survives today of the mill, the first factory in West Lothian. The site has not been built over and survives as a piece of open ground west of the Mill Road bridge. The outline of fallen rubble suggests where the walls may have stood. On a recent visit, a piece of the river embankment had fallen away, revealing the underlying soil. Some nine inches down could be seen a thin black layer – the soot of the 1877 fire.

The mill lade left the Almond at the former mill dam behind St Kentigern's Academy, and its course can be traced, though near Riddochhill Farm it has been built over. A sluice regulated the water level in the lade, and can be seen between Blackburn Villa and the footbridge to St Kentigern's.

The late 18th and early 19th century houses built to accommodate the mill workers were sold off after the fire, and over the years were gradually demolished and replaced. The mill manager's house – a stone villa among trees on Mill Road, built by Wallace the Blackburn masons probably in the late 1850s – was sold off in the early 1880s. The street names – Mill and Ladeside Roads – recall Blackburn's days as a textile village.

CHAPTER 9

Roads and Railways

GOOD COMMUNICATIONS, both road and rail, were important if a village was to develop into an industrial centre.

Along the new turnpike roads grew up businesses eager to profit from passing travellers – especially blacksmiths' workshops and inns. By 1773 Blackburn had the New Inn – the old Redhouse Farm. Behind it can still be seen the courtyard and stables where teams of horse were changed while travellers took refreshment. From c.1770 to 1840 was the heyday of the coaching era – when roads were good, and the railways had not yet arrived to steal their trade.

From 1805, two Royal Mail coaches passed through the village daily – to Edinburgh at three in the afternoon, and to Glasgow at half past two. (There was as yet no post office in Blackburn, so the mail coach dropped off Blackburn's post at Whitburn.) In addition, the 'Commercial' stagecoach passed through at half past six every evening, except Sunday; and the 'Rocket' from Hamilton to Edinburgh, three times a week at half-past eleven in the morning, and in the return direction at three in the afternoon. In 1908 an old Blackburn man could still remember the coaches with their drivers in tall hats and red coats, carrying hunting horns. 'Many a "hing" I had on the coaches. The Red Rover mail coach always came via the Blackburn road. The Halfway House between Whitburn and Harthill was where the coaches stopped for a change of horses. Occasionally the coaches on the Blackburn road and the Bathgate road held races, as the drivers could see one another far across the fields that separated the roads. Many a wager was won and lost as to which coach would reach Edinburgh first.' The owners of the stagecoaches on the two roads each claimed the shortest route. The dispute went to arbitration, where it was found that the difference over the 43 miles between Glasgow and Edinburgh was a mere 230 yards (the Bathgate route being the shorter).

By 1820, the New Inn had closed its doors and become a genteel farmhouse, so perhaps Blackburn benefited less than it might have from so many travellers whirling through the village in a cloud of dust or splatter of mud. After the closure of the New Inn, there was no coaching inn in Blackburn where the stagecoaches could stop and change horses. Later in the century, the Crown Inn and other local public houses would hire out a horse and carriage as required, but they were 'posting inns,' not 'coaching inns' of the stagecoach era.

18th and 19th century housing on the north side of East Main Street.
John McLaren

Blackburn's trade grew slowly. In 1825, a single carrier, Peter Mair, went weekly to Glasgow from Blackburn on Thursday, returning on Saturdays. Presumably, Blackburn Cotton Mill and the Flax Works had their own carts to bring in the raw material, and take away the finished yarn. By 1837, a daily carrier service operated to Edinburgh (except of course on the Sabbath), and a weekly service to Glasgow. All these services were a result of being on a well-maintained main road. Blackburn was by no means a rural backwater in the first half of the 19th century: it was a busy industrial community, on a main road between Scotland's two most important cities, and able to benefit by trading with both.

Today, the main road through Blackburn follows the route of the original turnpike road. At Mill Road, however, the turnpike took a turn to the north, so that it crossed the River Almond at right angles, making an easier task for the bridge-builder. In 1822 the main road was straightened by the addition of a new bridge over the Almond, replacing a ford. The odd little loop around Mill Road survives, as does the old bridge, now some 230 years old. The river at this point marks the boundary between Livingston and Whitburn parishes.

Rat(s) Road

Another old road still survives in Blackburn – the Rat(s) Road, which goes south from the main road, opposite the foot of Mill Road. Why it was given that name is not known for certain; perhaps it refers to the people who used this side road to avoid paying tolls on the turnpike road! It was the main road to West Calder until the 1840s, when only a few hundred yards of new road and a bridge had to be built, to create the present, more direct route from the Cross to West Calder. The Rat(s) Road can be followed on foot today, though it is very overgrown. Its continuation to the east is now the track to Blackburnhall Farm.

Railway transport – cheap, fast and comfortable – immediately killed off passenger coach transport by road. The railway boom began in the 1840s and continued for half a century, until the whole country was covered with a network of lines. In 1845, a railway was proposed 'from the Edinburgh and Glasgow Railway near Ratho Station to the Town of Bathgate,' with branches to Whitburn, Blackburn, Binny Quarries, and Mid Calder. From Barracks Farm, south east of Bathgate, a line would have passed west through Blackburn and Whitburn, joining up with the Airdrie and Bathgate Railway Company's proposed route. The route was one of a proliferation of railway schemes, many of which, including this one, never came to fruition. So although, misleadingly, it appears on the A. & C. Black map of Linlithgowshire in 1847, it was unfortunately never built, for it might have made a great difference to Blackburn's future.

However, there were several stations within a couple of miles of the village: in 1849, the Edinburgh and Bathgate railway line opened; in 1850, East Whitburn Station opened on the Wilsontown, Morningside and Coltness line; in 1869, West Calder Station opened on the Cleland line; and mineral lines later led in to Riddochhill and Whitrigg collieries.

CHAPTER 10

Blackburn House after 1845

DESPITE THE FAILURE OF James Sceales' flax business at Hopefield Mill and the Mill of Blackburn, another member of the family was willing to try his luck in Blackburn. In 1845, Blackburn House and estate were bought by Andrew Sceales of Jamaica Street, Leith. He was probably the brother of James Sceales; perhaps he hoped to save the flax business, which was still owned by James Sceales' trustees at this time.

Blackburn House was Andrew Sceales' residence for only a few years, for he died at the age of 70 in 1851. His widow Euphemia lived there for another ten years until her death. Her trustees then let Blackburn House to a succession of tenants.

John Pender (1815–1896)
West Lothian Council Libraries

In 1871, Blackburn House was bought by John Pender, a self-made man and a well-known figure in Victorian times. Born in Glasgow in 1816, he made a fortune in textiles, and then became a pioneer of submarine telegraphy. He was wealthy enough to put up security for a quarter of a million pounds, thus enabling his company to lay a telegraph cable across the Atlantic, and later to India, Asia, Australasia and Africa. He stood unsuccessfully for Parliament in Linlithgowshire in 1868, but thereafter served several terms as MP for Totnes and for Wick Burghs. In 1888, he was knighted for his services to the Empire.

As well as Blackburn House, he also owned Middleton Hall in Uphall, and his initials can be seen on Muir's Buildings (west of the Oatridge Hotel) in Uphall. However, he lived mainly in London, so his Blackburn and Uphall properties lay empty. In 1886, the *West Lothian Courier* described Blackburn House as 'once a charming spot with its trim policies and walks, its fine garden and mansion.' But it had 'changed hands so often, that each change seems to be for the worse: a Dead Sea dissolution seems to hang around it, and the cheery life which made music within its walls, and the genial hospitalities dispensed under its roof, seem to have departed for ever.'

However, in 1889, Blackburn House was let to Thomas Forsyth as tenant farmer, whose family connection with it was to last for over 50 years. During the Second World War, after the death of Thomas' widow, Catherine Forsyth, the house was sold by the trustees of the Pender estate (who still owned it long after Sir John's death in 1896). A succession of owners – John Walker, John Whitelaw, Robert Russell – struggled to maintain the mansion house on the profits from its small farm. The house was A-listed in 1971, but ceased to be lived in about 1973 when Robert Russell moved into a modern bungalow to the west of the mansion house. After a century of slow decline, when its owners were absentees or small farmers lacking the means to keep up a mansion house, Blackburn House was left to decay for three decades, a victim of damp, rot and vandalism.

The property was split up yet again, with the mansion and its fields bought by Frank Kennedy, while the modern bungalow went to another owner. Mr Kennedy wanted the fields for a riding school, but the derelict mansion which came with them soon proved a major headache. West Lothian district council pressed him to make the house wind and watertight, but even the most basic protective measures were estimated at several thousand pounds. Full restoration was far beyond his means.

When a building preservation body expressed interest in acquiring the House, Mr Kennedy was glad to get it off his hands. The house was sold for a nominal sum to the Blackburn House Preservation Trust and the Architectural Restoration and Conservation Organisation of Scotland. Their plan was to turn it into a Scottish National Centre for Architectural Conservation, and to use unemployed people as the workforce while training them in the skills of building, restoration and conservation. Financial and other support was given by the Department of Employment, the European Social and Regional Development Fund, and the Bank of Scotland.

Despite its poor condition, there was general agreement that the house was worth saving. In 1991, architect James Simpson judged it to be:

> certainly in the second rank of architecturally important small country houses, on a par with Aberdeen's Haddo House ... Houses of this period and quality are rare in any part of Scotland. Certainly if Blackburn House had been in some pretty part of Perthshire or East Lothian ... it would not have been allowed to deteriorate to its present state. However the house would most probably have been extended and altered if it had been in either of these two locations.

Unfortunately the project soon ran into difficulties: within a few months of starting in 1993, it foundered, and the Bank of Scotland repossessed the house in lieu of some £40,000 owed by the Trust. Once again the house mouldered, with vandals frustrating all efforts to keep the fabric wind and watertight.

Blackburn House from the south, 2002
Eva Kennedy

Then in 2000, thanks to the persistence of West Lothian council's conservation officer, Stuart Eydmann, the Cockburn Conservation Trust began to take an interest in the House. Three years of preparing feasibility studies, devising a viable use for the house, and putting together a complex funding package, reached a successful conclusion. £3 million of funding were secured, and restoration work is to begin on the house in late 2005.

Funding

The funders are the Heritage Lottery Fund (£1,827,000), Historic Scotland (£500,000), the European Regional Development Fund (£740,000), Scottish Enterprise Edinburgh and Lothians (£200,000), and West Lothian council (£47,500). The Bank of Scotland generously agreed to hand over the building to the Cockburn Conservation Trust for the sum of £1, and to sponsor the new users of the House for five years.

When the restoration is complete, the Cockburn Conservation Trust will lease the building to Caledonian Arthouse, which will provide serviced business units for lease to creative artists, musicians, and businesses. The two main rooms (the former drawing and dining rooms) will be restored without modern intrusions such as fluorescent lighting, and will be available for functions and marketing events, and also for location filming where a period setting is required. The basement and upper stories will be let as small business units.

The work of restoration (under architects Simpson and Brown) will include rebuilding the demolished west pavilion and doocot to restore the symmetry of the house. The original lime render will be reapplied. The fine interior plasterwork of the main public rooms will be saved and conserved as far as is possible. The former chief planner with West Lothian district council, George McNeill, has been instrumental in bringing the project to fruition, and will oversee the restoration to its hoped-for completion in 2007.

An important part of the Caledonian Arthouse ethos is community involvement: each firm or individual who leases part of the premises will be required to lend its talents each year to local community projects. In addition, the restored west doocot will open to the public as a small heritage centre. The House will again become a focal point for Blackburn, a centre of economic and creative activity, and, it is hoped, a magnet to attract other new businesses to the area. In its new incarnation, however, the people of Blackburn will not be shut out, but will have the chance to visit, to appreciate the fine interior, and to benefit from the creative energy to be gathered there.

CHAPTER II

Newcomers to Blackburn

THE EARLIEST SETTLERS IN the new village of Blackburn in the 1770s were the residents of the old village. How many moved to New Blackburn, and how many had to leave the area, cannot now be known, but certainly some of the residents of the New Town were from the old village, and others came from no more than two or three miles away – Bathgate, Foulshiels, etc.

Roadmen at work on the road between Blackburn and Addiewell, 1890s. The wheeled machine scraped off the mud. The man in the centre is William Charge who came to Blackburn from Buckinghamshire c.1860.

Violet Carson

Once the Cotton Mill came into full production, incomers were attracted to Blackburn by the prospect of work. Houses were built by the Cotton Mill owners, and the workforce grew slowly. The opening of the flax spinning mill and canvas weaving workshop boosted the population in the 1820s and 1830s.

The first evidence of the origins of Blackburn's population is the 1841 census:

some 60 per cent were born in West Lothian; 40 per cent were born outside the county. Blackburn was growing not just by natural increase, but by immigration to the village.

At the end of the 1840s, Blackburn grew rapidly, with an influx of workers employed in the construction and operation of the Bathgate Chemical Works. The 1850s were more stable, but the 1860s were again a decade of growth. Mining brought the next influx of newcomers to the village. In the 1861 census, there were 32 coal mine workers in Blackburn: twelve were from Ireland, one from England, six from elsewhere in Scotland, and eight from surrounding parishes. Probably only five were Blackburn men, so it seems that coal mining held little attraction for local men while there was alternative employment. Thus in order to work their mines, the coal companies had to rely on incomers.

Irish Immigration

The first identifiable group of immigrants to Blackburn was the Irish, in the mid 19th century. In the 1840s the potato harvest in Ireland failed and millions were reduced to acute hunger and want. Many hundreds of thousands starved to death; well over a million emigrated in the six years following 1844; and over the next 70 years another six million left Ireland. Many of them came to Scotland.

Scotland was the nearest country to Ireland, and the easiest and cheapest destination from the north and west of Ireland. Wages in Scotland were far higher than in Ireland, and there were plenty of jobs in the growing industries of railways, mining, iron, steel and textiles. The work which the Irish took was generally unskilled and often temporary. After landing in Glasgow, the Irish arrivals gradually spread out eastward in stages, moving from job to job. Some were short-term immigrants, working only for the harvest season, or for a few years until they had saved some money and could go home again. Others stayed, settled and made a new life.

The arrival of the Irish in Blackburn began as a trickle and became a flood. In 1841, before the terrible famine, there were 25 Irish in Blackburn, out of a population of 443 (5.6 per cent). Three were labourers, nine worked in the Cotton Mill, and most of the rest were children. By 1851, seven years after the start of the famine, the number had shot up to 137 – 20 per cent of the total population, or one in five. They found work mainly as general or agricultural labourers. Seven adults and about fifteen youngsters were employed in the Cotton Mill. In the 1850s the number of Irish increased again to a peak in 1861 of 156 Irish-born, out of a total population of 758 (20.6 per cent).

The Irish were a mobile group. None of the Irish in Blackburn at the time of the 1841 census were still there in 1851; and only twenty or so of those in the 1851 census were still there in 1861, though some Irish girls may have married and changed their surnames, so cannot be traced from one census to the next. Thereafter they grew more settled, as second generation children grew up who had never known Ireland, and had put down roots in this country, integrating and perhaps intermarrying with the local community. Immigration continued, but on a much lesser scale after 1861. By 1891, there were 67 Irish-born out of a total Blackburn population of 814 (8 per cent).

Immigration to Scotland was made easier by 'chain migration': the first immigrants encouraged their families and friends to follow them, offered them accommodation and got them jobs. In Blackburn in 1851, nearly a third of the Irish were lodgers, almost all of them with fellow Irish families. One household, that of Peter O'Hara, a labourer, contained himself, his wife and five children, plus two lodgers and their families – a total of sixteen people in what was probably a two-roomed house. Some lodgers moved on or returned to Ireland; some settled down and found houses of their own.

The Irish population in Blackburn was much higher than in West Lothian as a whole: in 1851, 20 per cent in Blackburn, against 9.2 per cent in West Lothian as a whole; in 1871, 14.6 per cent in Blackburn, compared to 8 per cent in West Lothian. By the end of the century, the discrepancy was not so marked, but the questions arises as to why a disproportionately large number of Irish came to Blackburn.

Once a 'colony' of Irish was established, it became self-perpetuating to some extent, as each settled family encouraged others to join them. But to attract the first influx, there must have been both jobs and accommodation available. It may be that the closure of the flax spinning mill and canvas works had created a surplus of accommodation through the departure of redundant workers; and the Cotton Mill required a large number of unskilled workers, especially youngsters. Also the railways, Boghead coal mines, and the Bathgate Chemical Works (under construction by 1851) required a large pool of unskilled labour.

The most common jobs for Irish immigrants were in the Cotton Mill or in labouring, but by the 1860s coal mining was beginning to absorb a good many. Even as late as 1881, most were in coal mining and labouring, though a few were beginning to make their way into the skilled trades.

There was of course friction between Irish and Scots, given the huge and sudden influx. The main cause of resentment was that the Irish were happy to take jobs at less than the going rate – which was far higher than they could have dreamed of in Ireland. For most of the 19th century however, work in West

Lothian was plentiful, so the two groups were not often in competition for the same jobs. Sectarianism did rear its ugly head at times, as when a riot erupted in Bathgate between Irish and Scots in 1857; but the immigrants to West Lothian were overwhelmingly Catholic, so that Irish sectarian tensions were not generally imported with the newcomers. Those who came to Blackburn came to a village where there were plenty of jobs, and where almost every family lived in the same sort of accommodation, with the same limited income, so that ill feeling caused by economic disparity was absent. Most of the immigrants were young and adaptable; two thirds were male so intermarriage was not uncommon, and within a generation it must have been difficult to tell which families were of Irish origin.

Irish immigration continued on a much smaller scale into the 20th century. The latest figure from the 2001 census is 0.7 per cent Irish-born people living in Blackburn, fewer than the percentage born in England, or Continental Europe. Today, the population of Blackburn, ethnically, is remarkably *un*-diverse, with a mere 0.55 per cent born outside Europe.

CHAPTER 12

Coal Mining

THE DEVELOPMENT OF BLACKBURN from its first encounter with industry – the building of the Cotton Mill in 1794 – until the end of the 19th century, is easy to sum up. Until the Cotton Mill burnt down in 1877, it was a textile village. From then onwards, coal mining predominated.

The coal in the Blackburn area is part of the carboniferous limestone which runs south from Bathgate. In geological prehistory, the strata were 'invaded by hot tongues of molten whinstone in the form of dykes.' These faults caused great problems in coal mining, and could produce dangerous working conditions.

Heatherfield Fault

Former Blackburn miner Alex Russell points out that: 'Blackburn village sits squarely upon such a fault running from the Bathgate Hills in the North, to Woolfords and Tarbrax in the South. This fault is the Heatherfield Fault ... It has a tendency to come into full view and we can see this at the underpass at the former British Leyland site and again at the Trinleyknowe site ... It is near this point that the Fault throws a leg westwards ... This leg of the Fault was well known to local miners as it separated the coal workings of Riddochhill Colliery from the Latch and Whitrigg Collieries to the South. The village therefore sits astride the Heatherfield Fault, almost following the Bathgate Road.'

Blackburn lies over coal deposits which have been worked since at least the 18th century. The first person known to be active in mining in the Blackburn area was Alexander Cuthbertson, who was born in 1703. Though a poor boy, he gained an education and became factor to the Earl of Rosebery, the owner of the Livingston estate. He was commissioned by a group of landowners to exploit the coal and lime reserves on their estates, and sank several 'coal heughs' at Breichmill, Polbeth, Blackburn and Bo'ness. He may have lived to regret his efforts, when he fell down a shaft one dark night while riding home from Linlithgow. A 1766 writer reports:

> down he falls with his horse to the bottom ... and which was very remarkable, kept fixed in his saddle without being the least hurt, tho' the pit was near five fathom deep [30 feet] ... By the help of ropes and lights, [they] soon pulled both him and horse up, being more afraid than hurt.

Early mines were shallow because the technology to keep a deep mine free from water did not exist. The earliest coal workings were drained by digging a downward sloping adit (drain) from the coal seam to open ground. This depended on there being suitable low-lying ground nearby such as a river gorge or valley. Later, horse-drawn or water-powered endless chains were introduced, by which buckets scooped up the water at the pit bottom and emptied it at the top. Most early mines were no more than 80 feet deep and were generally simple bell-shaped pits. Even in the 1840s, the average number employed at a West Lothian coal mine was just 24. These small pits were soon worked out and abandoned, and new ones sunk. West Lothian is dotted with scores of these pits, whose whereabouts can sometimes be guessed by the presence of small craters left by their subsidence. There is often no other record of their existence, as the legal requirement to record mine shafts and workings was not introduced until the mid-19th century.

Throughout the 18th and 19th centuries there was an increasing demand for coal – both for domestic use and for growing industries like foundries, potteries, glass-works, breweries, salt pans and lime kilns. Some coal mines reached depths of as much as 240 feet, but encountered insuperable problems of bad drainage and ventilation. These problems were overcome by the gradual introduction of steam engines in the second half of the 18th century. Mines could now go ever deeper in the search for coal, and the technology was applied to drainage, ventilation and the winding gear used to raise the coal to the surface.

A steam engine was in use in a Blackburn pit by the early years of the 19th century. Exactly when it was installed is not known, but it was on land that was part of the Blackburn estate, so it was possibly during the ownership of Thomas Douglas, the coalmaster.

The shafts where these cumbersome steam engines operated were known as engine pits. Blackburn's engine pit lay to the south of the main road, at the south west edge of what is now Rattray Gardens. It was connected by underground workings to the working pit, which lay on the north side of the main road, an area still known to Blackburn residents at the Mine Plantin'.

An early writer on the mining industry in West Lothian, Charles Forsyth, wrote c.1846 that coal was at one time 'worked in the lands of Blackburnhall, where old workings were formerly seen in a freestone quarry near the Almond Water. Coal was also formerly worked at Hopefield, which was called Blackburn coal-work, and in the lands of Red House, where only the crop [outcrop] of the seam was worked.'

The 'Blackburn coal-work' was south of Blackburn House and the River Almond. 'About 33 fathoms (i.e. 200 feet) below the bed of limestone which has been worked at Blackburn, there is a bed of caking coal, six feet thick, having a thin seam of stone in the centre of it, which was formerly worked at Hopefield. This is the principal seam of the Blackburn coal-field and dips north west one foot in three. An engine was used for pumping the water. The unusual circumstance of limestone lying immediately above the coal, and forming the roof, here occurs.'

In addition to those mentioned by Forsyth, there was a small coal mine at the other end of the village, near the Cotton Mill. None of these mines was large, none could go very deep, and all had been abandoned by 1817. After this early period, coal mining ceased in Blackburn for about thirty or forty years. In the 1841 census, there was not a single miner in Blackburn; or to be more exact, there was one – a nine year-old boy called John Frame. The following year he would have been forbidden to work below ground, after the findings of a Royal Commission into the employment of women and children in mines shocked the public and forced politicians to ban the underground employment of women and young children.

Women at work in the mines, c.1840

First Report of the Royal Commission on the Employment of Children, 1842

An elderly Blackburn woman, Mrs John Sneddon, was interviewed by the *West Lothian Courier* in 1903. She had grown up in Bo'ness and as a nine-year-old girl was sent underground to work as a drawer for her father (carrying the coal from the face to the bottom of the shaft). To calm her fear of going down the 'black hole,' her older sister pretended she would see 'fine big apples growing on the trees down the pit; needless to say she got a sad disappointment for the only trees she saw were those used for propping up the roof of the road [passageway], and the apples were conspicuous by their absence.'

Mrs Sneddon was thirteen when the Coal Mines Act of 1842 was passed:

She remembered that many of the old female workers in the pits were lamenting the fact as to how they would get the wherewithal to live seeing that their mode of earning a living had been taken from them ... Such work was bad enough for men, but what must it have been for the women?

In 1851, there were only five miners in Blackburn, probably employed at the old

Polkemmet Pit, or at the Boghead mines supplying coal to the newly opened Bathgate Chemical (Oil) Works of James Young. By the time of the 1861 Census, there were 32 miners in Blackburn, but mining was still insignificant as an employer compared to the Cotton Mill. Naturally most of the miners lived at the west end of the village, closer to the pits in the Bathgate and Whitburn area.

In the 1860s, the shale industry began to develop at a terrific rate. James Young's patent ran out in 1864, and immediately a score of new companies were set up, all eager for a share of the huge profits to be made in oil. Blackburn was close enough to some of these works to benefit from their employment opportunities. By 1871, the shale industry employed 26 Blackburn men as miners, and 58 in oil works. At this point shale outranked coal in importance as an employer.

So, by 1871, mining had become significant in Blackburn's economy, and for the next century was to be Blackburn's most important employer. Mines had become deeper and larger, needing not just a few dozen men, but a workforce of many hundreds.

Ten years later, by 1881, coal had left shale far behind. However, in 1883, the Bathgate Oil Company began to operate the Seafield Oil Works. The village of Seafield developed at this time, with rows of houses to accommodate the workforce. It was later taken over by the Pumpherston Oil Company, which modernised Seafield Works in 1897, so that the shale industry continued to employ

Gavin Paul, the coalmaster who sank Riddochhill, Boghead and Mosside Collieries.

St John's Church, Bathgate

many Blackburn men. However, coal was now king in Blackburn. Gavin Paul & Sons, the coalmasters, had opened pits at Mosside and Boghead, which offered plenty of jobs, and by 1891, nearly half of Blackburn's working population was employed in mining.

The coal mines in the immediate vicinity of Blackburn were the Latchbrae – at the west end of the village – which was abandoned in 1875; Redhouse, which mined the Hurlet seam and was abandoned in 1908; the Almond Mines sunk by Gavin Paul & Sons, to the west of Riddochhill, a small mine employing fewer than 40 and abandoned in 1920; and Mosside, another Gavin Paul mine. From 1890, however, the two mines of most importance to Blackburn were Riddochhill and Whitrigg.

Riddochhill

Riddochhill was one of three collieries owned and operated by Gavin Paul & Sons, the others being Mosside and Boghead. Work began on the sinking of Riddochhill about 1888 and continued for several years. Coal was first struck in August 1891, by which time the pit was employing 119 miners. Ten years later, 250 were employed. Most of the coal found a market in the numerous shale oil works in the district.

One colliery could consist of several mines or pits, given different names or numbers. At Riddochhill, two new 'mines' were sunk in 1914, electrically powered and employing 100 men each.

During the First World War, mines were taken under government control, so that coal production for the war effort could be co-ordinated and maximised. At the end of the war, the mines were handed back to their owners. Faced with shrinking markets in Britain and overseas, owners cut wages. A national miners' strike began on 1 April 1921. The miners' case was a good one: the cost of living had risen to 141 per cent of prewar prices, and yet their wages were to be cut back to prewar rates. They called for the unification of the industry, for all mining company profits to be pooled, and for mining wages to be decided nationally.

By the third week of the strike, an estimated 1,000 marines and soldiers had been stationed in West Lothian, and every pit had armed guards to prevent damage

Marines who guarded Riddochhill Pit during the 1921 miners' strike.
David Hedges

or interference by the miners. To demonstrate their solidarity, 200 young men and boys from Blackburn and East Whitburn, some armed with cudgels and carrying red flags, marched to Bathgate, headed by East Whitburn Pipe Band. At the Steelyard, they noticed smoke issuing from Easton pit chimneys, and this betrayed the fact that the boilers were lit. The men marched to the pit, and a deputation of eight asked that the fires be put out. This was done and the men dispersed peaceably.

The strike brought hardship to the many families who lived from week to week, with no cushion of savings. In Blackburn, where over half the male working population was employed in the coal industry, four soup kitchens operated for over three months, supplying 800 children with dinner, six days a week. The money was raised through donations and public fund-raising – some £130 was needed every week; a large sum when most wage earners were on strike. Despite hardship, the miners held out until the beginning of July, but in the end were defeated. Their wages were cut and none of their demands were met.

The following year (1922), Gavin Paul & Sons sold Riddochhill to William Baird and Co., one of the largest firms in the Scottish coal and steel industries. The new owners decided to upgrade the pit – major work, requiring its closure for two years. The old shaft was stripped out and enlarged, new winding engines were installed, and the pithead was rebuilt and its operations were mechanised. Electrical machinery was installed underground: the coal was cut by Anderson and Boyes' chain machines and carried away on a Mavor and Coulsen Jigging Conveyor. When the work was finished, Riddochhill was one of the most up-to-date pits in the country.

By 1925, the economic situation was no better, and the coalmasters demanded an increase in miners' hours from seven to eight, and a further reduction in wages. Despite miners' protests, a Royal Commission backed the masters. Industrial action began on a scale never seen before or since. For nine days at the beginning of May 1926, every union came out in a General Strike in support of the mineworkers. Pickets attempted to prevent public transport services and goods deliveries by barricading roads. Between Blackburn and Swineabbey, a large tree was axed and allowed to fall across the road, and 20 telephone and telegraph wires were cut. A group of miners, 'armed with stones and other missiles, attempted to hold up a motor transport [lorry]' at Blackburn. Alexander MacLachlan and four others were arrested, and although they had believed they were following TUC instructions to check all vehicles, all five were convicted and fined.

For the miners, it was a long and bitter strike. The coalmasters refused to negotiate on a national basis, insisting that each area settle separately. District negotiations finally began in late November and the strike came to an end in late December, eight months after it had begun. The miners were defeated, wages were cut, and hours increased to prewar levels. The strikes caused great hardship in mining communities like Blackburn and left a legacy of bitterness and distrust. The suffering of these bleak years lives on in local folk memory – soup kitchens, lay-offs, dole queues, gnawing money worries, the Means Test humiliation, and idle men on street corners. Many in the industry became convinced that fair wages and conditions could only be gained if mines were removed from the private companies and nationalised.

For the coal companies too, the two decades between the wars were a difficult time. Markets were shrinking, competition from cheaper sources of coal increasing, and alternative sources of energy such as oil and hydroelectric power were coming into use. The coalmasters responded to these difficulties by increasing hours and cutting wages, but also by increasing efficiency. By 1937, 79 per cent of coal in Scotland was machine cut, far exceeding the British average of 57 per cent. Productivity rose, but was offset by the continued decline in coal prices.

Tragedy

In December 1933 a sad accident was reported at Riddochhill. 'Miners toiling in the gloom heard the dreaded rush which signifies a fall of coal and stone. There was silence which was broken by a voice – praying. It was the voice of a young miner buried under the fall. The voice guided them as they worked feverishly to extricate him. They cleared his head and body. Still the debris about his feet held him prisoner. 'Are you there, boys?' he called. The rescue squad redoubled their efforts. There came another ominous sound. The miners jumped for safety – just in time. Another fall buried the trapped miner completely. He was dead when extricated. The victim was Patrick Boyle, aged 23, who resided with his father at Paulville, Bathgate, and was employed at Riddochhill.'

The economic situation only began to improve with rearmament in the mid-1930s. By 1938, Riddochhill was thriving, and new pithead baths were provided by the Miners' Welfare Committee – a national organisation with an active West Lothian branch. As well as baths and showers, the building provided 256 pit-clothes lockers, and another 256 clean clothes lockers, 'the latest mechanical boot cleaning apparatus,' and a first aid room and canteen. The upkeep of the baths was met by a levy from the men's wages. As one of the speakers at the official opening pointed out, 'the benefit would not be felt so much at the pit as in their homes by their wives and families.'

At the outbreak of war in 1939, the Government again took over direction of the country's mines. The intensity of the war effort created a huge demand for coal, but little investment in the mines, so it was a run-down, old-fashioned industry that was nationalised by Attlee's Labour government in 1947.

High expectations of nationalisation among the miners gave way quickly to disillusionment. Distrust of the private companies was rapidly replaced by distrust of the National Coal Board (NCB). In 1948, 400 miners at Riddochhill Colliery came out on unofficial strike over the withdrawal of a temporary allowance.

The NCB had eventually to grasp the nettle of under-investment and uneconomic pits, and in the Scottish Division, 140 collieries closed in a mere 14 years. Others were modernised, and new pits were opened. At first it seemed that Riddochhill would be one of the lucky ones.

Joseph Dawson

In 1951, Joseph Dawson was appointed manager of Riddochhill. He was said to have been a manager of outstanding ability; certainly he had a good opinion of his own merits, declaring at his retirement that he had 'been down big pits in many parts, including England, but I've never seen any better run than Riddochhill.' Dawson was a tough manager – 'He could tear you to ribbons' – but he earned the unions' respect. 'A chief characteristic of Mr Dawson during any dispute had been his overpowering determination to have production resumed at once, no matter whose toes were to be trodden on.'

In 1951, Riddochhill was producing 200–300 tons daily. In 1955, the NCB installed there the first Joy Continuous Miner in Scotland, a coal-cutting machine which could work in low seams without drilling and blasting. To cope with the increased output, the shafts were enlarged and fitted with two and a half ton capacity skips in place of cages and tubs. In 1958, a record output was attained, thanks to further reconstruction by the NCB. Two underground mines were driven to develop the Boghead area to the north west of the colliery, and their good quality coking coal was in demand for the manufacture of coke in Scottish steel works. In 1960, Riddochhill was fully mechanised and switched to producing coal for Braehead power station.

Production per manshift broke the 40 cwt barrier. 'Riddochhill,' reported the NCB's *Coal News,* 'is a pit where you can sense immediately the interest taken in the colliery's future. As men reach the surface after their stint, they often ask how many hutches came up during their shift... Having experienced working in a fully mechanised colliery, none of the Riddochhill men would care to go back to the conventional methods.'

In 1962, the NCB declared Riddochhill a category A pit – one with a long life ahead of it. It seemed that the great efforts made by manager and men had earned the pit a secure future. By 1966, annual output was between 800 and 900 tons a day, and the workforce had a confident outlook. But despite the huge effort, it was barely two years later that the NCB announced that Riddochhill was to close. The *West Lothian Courier* reported the news on 23 February 1968:

Riddochhill Colliery
Crown Copyright

Riddochhill Colliery, Blackburn, is to close on 10th May this year ... The closure affects 460 workers, many of whom have been employed all their working lives at the colliery which has been in operation for over seventy years ... Riddochhill at present employs some 490 men, most of them resident in Blackburn, where for many years the colliery had been the village's main source of employment.

Union officials travelled to London to appeal to the NCB against closure. They were told that Riddochhill had lost £45,000 in each of the two previous years, and during the first half of 1967–68 output had slumped to just over 500 tons a day. 'The pit's chief coal reserves are under the industrial area of Armadale, and to avoid subsidence damage, there is only partial extraction and the coal has been more faulted than expected.'

Closure was deferred until July, then till September, to give the pit a chance to pay. To stay open, the colliery would have to produce 730 tons daily. In fact, the axe was stayed for another few months, but closure finally came on 6 December 1968. It was hoped that the remaining West Lothian pits would be able to absorb some Riddochhill men, though the large number of closures in the previous twenty years meant that the remaining collieries could scarcely take in any more men. Riddochhill itself in the 1950s had taken in miners from the west, some of whom had settled in Blackburn and were now being made redundant for a second time. Some jobs were offered at more distant pits, with transport provided. For the older men, however, prospects were bleak, and many never worked again.

Whitrigg

Whitrigg Colliery lay between Blackburn and Whitburn – at East Whitburn – but most of its miners' houses were built in Blackburn, and many of its workers were Blackburn men.

The sinking of Whitrigg was begun about 1900 by Robert Forrester and Co., a Glasgow coal company. At Whitrigg, the first mines to be developed were the Latch (Nos. 1 and 2) and Burnbrae (No. 4), a small drift mine entered by a long, steeply sloping tunnel. The Lady Pit, also called the Dales (No. 5), was begun in 1908. The cutting of the first sod took place on 24 March 1908. A large party of local dignitaries arrived and the ceremony took place in pouring rain. As the ground on which the mine was to be sunk was part of the Polkemmet estate, Lady Baillie had been invited to attend but 'owing to the inclemency of the weather,' she called off. Nevertheless the pit was named in her honour. The first sod was cut by Mrs Forrester, probably the mother of the company director, using an ordinary spade. A silver-mounted spade was presented to her as a memento of the occasion. Either the spade was large or the writing was small, for it bore a surprisingly detailed inscription: 'Presented to Mrs M. Forrester by Messrs Robert Forrester and Company Limited on the occasion of her cutting the first sod of the No. 5 Pit, Whitrigg Collieries, which is expected to be about 180 fathoms deep, by 21 feet by 10½ feet, and is to wind 100 tons of coal per hour.'

Whitrigg at this time was achieving an average output of 1,700 tons a day, and it was hoped that the Lady would add another 1,000 tons a day. Water caused the pit sinkers a great deal of difficulty. Pumping by steam power was inadequate and an electric pumping plant had to be brought in. In May 1912, at a depth of over 160 fathoms (860 feet), the Jewel coal seam was reached, and the sinkers hoisted a flag to tell the good news to the neighbourhood. Sinking continued until the Wilsontown Main seam was reached, some 1,000 feet below ground.

Disaster

'FATAL ACCIDENT – About one o'clock on Monday morning, while James Cuthbert, miner, was engaged in his work at No. 2 Whitrigg Colliery, near Blackburn, a large quantity of rock suddenly fell away from the roof, whereby Cuthbert received a compound fracture of the skull, with fractures of the right arm, leg and breast-bone. From the nature of the injuries, death appears to have been instantaneous. Deceased, who was 30 years of age, has been about Blackburn all his life. He leaves a widow and six of a family, with whom much sympathy is felt.' (1910)

Whitrigg had been troubled from its earliest days by blackdamp. Pockets of this poisonous gas could cause an explosion, so its detection led to lay-offs while it was dispersed. Forrester & Co. made extensive improvements to the ventilation in 1911, which solved the problem. That same year, Whitrigg was paying higher rates than any other local colliery and was taking on another 100 men.

Whitrigg Colliery Mine Rescue Team at the Scottish Mine Rescue Team Championships, 1961. Left to right: William Scott (captain), Alex Russell, Walter Goodfellow (later a teacher at St Kentigern's Academy), Geordie Russell, Harry Reston (junior).

Alex Russell

Miners at Whitrigg Colliery, 1950s.
West Lothian Council Museums

These years were the heyday of the mining industry. Employment was plentiful, output high, and demand steady. After the First World War, however, Whitrigg encountered the same difficulties as Riddochhill and the rest of the coal mining industry. In 1921, nearly 200 men were made idle when the Latch was temporarily shut down. The national strike of that year caused great hardship. When a settlement was reached after three months, the Lady Pit had to be pumped out, so it was still another four or five weeks before the 200-300 Whitrigg men could resume work. In 1923, there was a further downturn in trade. Thirty men were made idle when the Latch closed for a time. The national strike of 1926 brought much bitterness, and the rest of the 1920s and early 1930s were a dreary period of lay-offs, disputes, low coal prices and low wages.

By 1934, Whitrigg was recovering: some 600 men were employed, and a new mine, Burnbrae (the old Burnbrae mine had long since ceased to be worked), was being driven down to the China seam. Rearmament, then the coming of the Second World War, created renewed demand for coal, and for a time the industry was in full employment, selling immediately all the coal it could produce.

Further Disaster

August 1942 saw perhaps the saddest week in Whitrigg's history, when three mineworkers were killed in two separate accidents. Patrick Ryan (63) a labourer, was 'at work on the redd bing at Whitrigg Colliery, East Whitburn... when he was found to be missing. A search was made for him and the next day his body was discovered about 2 feet 6 inches below the redd. It is presumed that he pulled the pin out of a hutch which caused it to empty and he was caught in the rush of debris, about 3 tons in weight.'

Three days later, Robert Stronach (32) and George Dummond (36) were at work in Burnbrae Mine when they were pinned beneath a fall of roof. 'Workmates worked for five hours before Drummond was extricated, and an hour later they managed to extricate Stronach.' Both were dead. They left two widows and six children.

'PIT BOY KILLED – While working on Friday in No. 3 Whitrigg Colliery, East Whitburn, Patrick Graham (14), pithead worker, who lived with his parents at Riddochhill Crescent, Blackburn, was instantly killed when he fell amongst some machinery. As a mark of respect the colliery, which employs 1400 men, was idle on Saturday. The boy started work only three months ago.' (1944)

In 1947, with nationalisation, the long association of Whitrigg with Robert Forrester & Co. came to an end. It had been a close and active relationship, though sometimes difficult. After nationalisation, the future looked hopeful for Whitrigg. The colliery was believed to have a working life of another 50 years. By 1955, the workforce had risen to some 1,300 – more than twice the number employed at Riddochhill – and daily output was 1,600 tons, making it one of the largest collieries in West Lothian. Its underground workings were extensive, so that the coalface could be as much as two and a half miles from the bottom of the shaft. At the surface, there was a large complex of buildings: coal preparation, steam raising and power generating plants, and engineering shops for maintenance of the mining machinery, as well as an aerial ropeway for the disposal of discard and ash from the boilers. Pollution was a problem at Whitrigg, and an apparatus was installed for extracting the ash and dirt which generally went up with the smoke from the chimney. In addition, the bing burned, and if the wind was in the wrong direction, the smoke from it could be sucked down the main shaft by the ventilation system, and the pit had to be closed.

Explosions

Fortunately both Riddochhill and Whitrigg were relatively free of gas, so explosions, with their greater loss of life, were rare. However, in 1954, an explosion of fire-damp in the northside working of the main coal seam at Whitrigg resulted in injuries to eight miners: Alex Blackwood, Michael Fleming, Jan Szok and Blazy Rystard of Blackburn; and four Whitburn men. The explosion caused their clothes to catch fire, resulting in serious burns. To get to the surface, they had to be helped by their workmates for about a mile up a steep incline. 'In actual fact,' said a Coal Board official, 'nearly all the injured were stretcher cases, but they just refused to be carried.' Such was the character of the men who worked the mines in the Blackburn area.

Despite nationalisation, industrial relations at Whitrigg were not good. A week-long strike in 1955 in support of 15 coal face workers caused a loss of output of nearly 8,000 tons. Whitrigg survived the early pit closures of the 1950s, but in 1965 it was earmarked for early closure because its production was well below average. Dismayed by the news, both management and men accepted the need for change in order to save their jobs. Huge efforts resulted in a rise to 41 cwt per manshift – well above the Scottish average, and especially remarkable as the colliery was working a very narrow seam. The *West Lothian Courier* editor, Bob Findlay, a former miner, toured Whitrigg in 1968 and was impressed with the level of mechanisation:

> Where have all the shovels gone? In my three-hour tour of the colliery I scarcely saw one, or that equally diabolical instrument of torture, the pick. At the face, height is reduced to 33 inches, which means there is no alternative to getting down on your knees or on your back. I chose to crawl in to see the power loader at work plus the shearing machine which is the coal-winner. It travels along a 200 yard face cutting the coal as it goes and automatically ploughs it on to the loader.
>
> It is difficult to get in and out since there is barely room to crawl past the hydraulic jacks supporting the roof. I was an old-fashioned miner in that I had no experience of mechanised mining. Our greatest aid was our ears, for with them we could judge the 'crush' on the timbers and know when to stay in or get out. In mechanised mining, however, nothing can be heard above the noise of the machinery ... Therefore it was a matter of building up confidence in the steel, and with older miners especially, this took a long time.

Bob Findlay contrasted the old-style mine manager with the new. The old 'ruled his empire from the office chair and spent much of his time arguing with dissatisfied men, usually about money and why they couldn't get this or that. And he held the ultimate weapon – the sack, and that was much more potent than it is today. To think of joking with the manager was akin to getting familiar with the King.' The new manager was typified by Mr Pettigrew of Whitrigg who 'had a word and a joke with everyone he met. His aim is to take the men as much as possible into his confidence and keep them in the picture as far as the pit is concerned.'

The new style of collaborative management raised morale as well as output, but it was not enough to save the pit. The National Coal Board had already begun to run down the pit long before it closed. In 1968 the new section of the M8 motorway severed the branch railway into Whitrigg. The coal washer plant was abandoned, and the coal was taken to Polkemmet or to Easton for processing. The final closure came on 16 June 1972, due, the NCB claimed, to 'exhaustion of reserves.'

The sites of Riddochhill and Whitrigg collieries have been cleared and planted with trees. The M8 motorway crosses part of the former Riddochhill site, and water from the abandoned workings was used at the British Leyland truck plant at Bathgate. The Riddochhill bing continued to burn, emitting low levels of hydrogen sulphide with its characteristic odour of rotten eggs. Although the bing has now been partially removed, and the waste spread out over a wide area to form a plateau some ten metres above the original ground level, the fumes remain a problem. Continuing negotiations should result in its complete removal, extraction of the remaining coal reserves, and the rehabilitation of the ground. The site has been identified in the Local Plan as suitable for large-scale distribution development.

Sectarianism is said to have permeated the mines pre-nationalisation, with some claiming that 'it was mostly Catholics at Riddochhill,' whereas 'almost every manager at Whitrigg was a mason' – so if you were in the masons, you got a job there. Nor was racism unknown; Forrester at Whitrigg is said to have refused to employ Poles: 'Plenty of our own wanting jobs,' was his alleged view. At the end of the Second World War, the Polish forces resettlement camp was at Polkemmet estate. (During the conflict, the Polish officers had acquired a romantic image, and it was said that the fence at Polkemmet wasn't to keep the men in: it was to keep the women out.) After the war, the NCB took on about 150 Poles at Whitrigg and many got houses in Blackburn. It's said that the Whitrigg clerks couldn't spell the Polish names, so they gave them numbers. Naturally, the Polish miners resented it, so some of them changed to Scottish names, and if they married Scottish girls, some took their wife's name.

In the late 1950s, 760 Blackburn men were employed in mining. Within the five years from 1968 to 1972 inclusive, some 1,500 mining jobs were lost in the

Blackburn area. A few men were absorbed into the surviving pits – Easton and Polkemmet. Some of the younger men were able to retrain for jobs at British Leyland or in Livingston New Town. For most of the older men, it was the end of their working lives.

Village life revolved round the two pits. Older people recall the days when the Riddochhill Pit trip to Port Seton needed a fleet of ten double-decker buses and twenty-one single-deckers. Some retired miners speak with nostalgia of their mining days, but perhaps what they regret is the camaraderie, the community spirit, the sense of shared danger, skill, and strength. Ask them if, given their time again, they would go down the pit, and they shake their heads. Mining was a dangerous occupation, as Jim Wallace, superintendent of the baths and the first aid station at Whitrigg Colliery had cause to know. In his 35 years, he dealt with the corpses of 22 men killed in the pit, and treated a greater number with major injuries. Coalmining was a hard taskmaster that bred strong men and tightknit communities.

Riddochhill Fatalities in the First 20 Years

24 September 1891 John Marshall (19) pit bottomer
19 May 1894 Alex Thomson (53) miner
1 July 1895 William Smith (29) brusher
8 August 1901 Peter Connelly (28) miner
13 February 1904 Peter Aitken Jr. (14) trimmer
11 May 1905 Michael Reilly (35) roadsman
9 October 1905 Malcolm Wilson (28) miner
2 July 1906 James Forrest (38) miner
26 March 1907 John Walker (54) miner
19 September 1907 Henry McDonald (49) miner
5 April 1911 John Rodgers (51) miner

Whitrigg Fatalities in the First 20 Years

29 January 1900 Alexander Rogers (43) sinker
2 July 1900 George McCallum (33) drawer
31 January 1902 John Brash (37) miner
25 January 1904 Peter Connoly (17) drawer
19 April 1905 Smith Tennant (47) miner
27 January 1905 Hugh Brannan (29) miner
4 April 1910 James Cuthbert (30) miner
24 April 1912 John Hannah (55) miner
21 August 1913 William Kennedy (47) fireman

Number of Employees

	Riddochhill			Whitrigg	
1914	Gavin Paul & Sons	261		Forrester & Co.	483
1921	"	427		"	487
1924	Wm Baird & Co.	252		"	453
1934	"	261		"	728
1948	National Coal Board	385		National Coal Board	928
1950	"	455		"	1027
1953	"	508		"	1208
1960	"	680		"	1076
1968	"	468		"	-
1970	Closed			"	635

CHAPTER 13

Other Industries

Lime

LIME WAS WORKED IN Blackburn for less than a century and was never a large industry. Demand for lime grew in the 18th century – mainly as a fertiliser; but also as a cementing agent for the building industry, and a flux in iron works.

Lime crops out in the form of limestone; if near the surface it can be quarried; if underground it can be mined. In the Blackburn area, it was quarried, then taken to kilns east of the Mill of Blackburn. The kilns were generally built into the side of rising ground, and were brick-lined and stone-faced. The limestone was loaded into the kilns at the top, in layers with coal. It was set alight and burned for perhaps 24 hours, then the burnt lime was raked out through a drawhole at the base of the kiln, protected from wind and rain by being set back within a deep archway.

Limestone was usually exploited by being leased to an entrepreneur who then bore the cost of building and operating the kilns. John Williams, writing in April 1793, mentions 'the thin limestone, which was wrought lately by Captain Clarkson'; that is, Thomas Clarkson Moncrieff. Again, this merely indicates that he leased the lime on his estate. When James Bristow Fraser rouped the fields round Blackburn House in 1812, the terms of the lease included the right to work lime only from 'the old lime quarry of Blackburn to the north of the great road, opposite the present lime kiln.' This quarry was across the main road from the Wester Breich road end. The lime quarry and kilns were no longer working by 1846, because the 'dip' (the slope of the limestone seam) made working the lime unproductive.

Quarrying

Quarrying employed a handful of men in Blackburn in the mid 19th century. A whinstone quarry was in operation for some time, but had been abandoned before the middle of the 19th century, and is now the site of the Bathgate Family Centre at Trinleyknowe. A sandstone quarry was worked for a time, but its location is not known.

A more unusual type of stone crops out just south of the Almond – lakestone.

In geological terms, lakestone is an intrusion – molten rock forced up by subterranean eruption through existing rocks. It is a picrite, found in only three or four other places in Scotland. Lakestone was useless for building as it crumbled when exposed to damp, but because of its heat-resisting properties, it was highly prized for lining bakers' ovens and furnaces. (The original spelling was always 'leckstone,' but this term was subsequently dropped in favour of 'ovensole' or 'ovenstone.') About 1840, the lakestone quarry was one of James Sceales' business ventures, and employed half-a-dozen men. By 1843, the writer of the New Statistical Account reported that 'quarrying [was] now given up for encroaching on the public road.' The quarry was on Blackburn Mains Farm, so was probably given up when the new stretch of road connecting the Main Street to the Stoneyburn road was built.

By 1855, work had resumed on the lakestone to the east of the new stretch of road, under Richard Wallace and Son, a Blackburn family with varied business interests – quarry masters, builders, grocers, blacksmiths, bakers, confectioners and innkeepers. The stone was in demand and in the 1850s was reported by the *West Lothian Courier* to be sent to all parts of Scotland; and as far afield as America, Australia and New Zealand by 1877.

In 1877, a tragedy befell the Wallace family. The body of Peter Wallace was found in a water hole at the lakestone quarry. 'Deceased was in the habit of taking charge of the pumping engine during the night, and he is supposed to have lost his footing and fallen down into the water, which is 12 feet deep, striking his head on a projecting stone in the descent.'

For a time in the 1880s, lakestone was also worked at East Foulshiels by another Blackburn man, James Smith. This quarry had a short life, but the Wallaces continued to operate the one at Blackburn Mains until 1914, when it ceased to be a working quarry. It has been filled in.

Shale Oil

Blackburn is generally associated with coal, but it lies on the western edge of the West Lothian shale field. John Pender, the absentee owner of Blackburn House, built a Patent Fuel Works on his Seafield Farm about 1877. For some six years it lay idle and unlet; then in 1883 Pender set up a company – the Bathgate Oil Company Ltd – and leased to it the shale on his Blackburn and Seafield lands and the Seafield Patent Fuel Works. None of the shareholders were local men – none local even to West Lothian – though the manager, William Turnbull, lived briefly at Blackburn House.

The venture was short-lived. In October 1885, the directors declared that 'the

Company cannot by reason of its liabilities, continue its business, and it is advisable to wind up the same.' The company's assets, including the Seafield Oil Works, were taken over by the much larger and more successful Pumpherston Oil Company in 1892, and thereafter the shale industry flourished in Seafield for some forty years.

Fireclay

Whitrigg Fireclay mine lay between the Lady Pit and the main road, and was worked first by the Flemington Coal Company, then, after nationalisation of the coal mines, by a variety of firms. After 1953, its low-iron fireclay was used to make saggars – the protective boxes in which ceramic ware is fired. Charles Lindsay, mine deputy, was killed there in 1957 by a roof fall. A former Whitburn town councillor and treasurer, he was the son of the well-remembered Granny Lindsay who had the little cottage (originally the schoolmaster's house) between the Gospel Hall and the Masonic Hall. The mine was never a large concern and closed in the 1970s.

The Peat Mosses

Swineabbey Bridge
Jean Fooks

Peat mosses surrounded Blackburn from earliest times, and survive to this day. Easter Inch Moss lies to the east, and Blackburn Moss to the north west on the ill drained land between Blackburn and Mosside Farm. Blackburn Moss was the 'Commonty of Blackburn' – or Blackburn Common.

A common is often thought to have been land owned in common by all the residents of a village. In fact, a common was privately owned land, over which the owners' tenants, cottars and labourers had certain rights. Blackburn Common comprised land owned by at least four different landowners. The tenants of each of these landowners had the right to graze their animals there – though being moss, it must have offered poor grazing. A document of 1769 records that the tenants of Little Blackburn had the right of digging peats from the moss. Tenants also had the right to dig up turf (for roofing) from the Common. The fact that it was important to the tenants all around it, may well explain the existence of the Swineabbey Bridge. It was not, as it looks nowadays, a bridge to nowhere: it was a bridge to the Common, by which the tenants of Blackburn and Pottishaw, laden with creels of turf or peat, crossed the Almond. In 1802, the rights to Blackburn Common were said to have been 'enjoyed as Commonty for forty years bygone or past memory of man' and consisted of the right of 'pasturing cattle, casting feal [turf] and divot, and using other acts of common property therein...'

In 1802, William Honyman (Lord Armadale) and Thomas Mair of Pottishaw raised a summons in law to force their fellow owners, Alexander Russell of Mosside, William Dick of Standhill, James Ranken of Inchcross, and Mr Tenant, owner of part of Wester Inch, to agree to divide up the Common. Similar instances were taking place all over Britain between about 1750 and 1850: common ground was divided up among the various landowners, fenced off, drained, and brought into use as pasture or arable. The ordinary people lost their rights of grazing or peat cutting, making life still harder for the poor. Despite a claim by Russell of Mosside that most of the Common belonged to him, the courts gave permission for the land to be divided up among all the landowners in proportion to their existing holdings, and for march-stones to be set up to show the boundaries of each owner's section.

Moss Litter

Moss litter companies flourished in West Lothian, with operations at Bathgate, Fauldhouse and Armadale. At first the moss litter (dried peat) was used for horse and cattle bedding, but various uses evolved: as fertiliser in agriculture and horticulture; as a filler for molasses in cattle feed; as poultry bedding; and in a pulverised and granulated form, it was used in the manufacture of explosives and the refining of coal gas. Peat could also be used in the making of magnesium alloy for the manufacture of metals, and during the Second World War, much peat went into aircraft production. Only the upper sphagnum layer was taken. The deeper peat, suitable for burning as fuel, was seldom used.

In the 1920s, the Moss Litter Company of Edinburgh was working the peat moss immediately north of Riddochhill Colliery. The larger East Inch Moss had begun to be exploited about 1916 when it was leased by the Midland Moss Litter Company of Glasgow. The company built four houses for its key workers at the east end of Blackburn. The workers were Dutch; they were often recruited by moss litter firms as they had expertise in working boggy land reclaimed from the sea.

Dutch Cottages

The earliest Dutch workers in Blackburn were G. Van Tersal, Maninus Kieviets, Johann van Doren and Antoon Tabor, and their houses became known as the Dutch cottages – they were almost the last cottages on the right on the Seafield road. The early workers came and went, spending a few years in Blackburn before returning to Holland. After the First World War, they tended to stay for longer periods; indeed Johannes van Tongerloo and Hendrick Schuttert spent much of their working lives in Blackburn, while Johanna de Graaf, widowed in the 1920s, was still living in one of the Dutch cottages nearly 30 years later, and some descendants still live in Seafield. The company continued to operate on Easter Inch Moss until about 1956, and the Dutch Cottages were sold off about 1960 to James Danskin, who converted them into two houses.

The peat was dug, stacked and left to dry. Then it was taken to a factory on the moss, where it was crushed and baled. The bales of peat were brought from the moss by a horse-drawn tramway, and older residents recall that on the site of some of the Beechwood Road flats, stood the peat receiving deck, where the peat was stacked ready for distribution by lorry. Until the closure of the Seafield Oil Works in 1931, a branch line came off the Bathgate railway line right into the Midland Moss Litter Works, then on to the Seafield Works. The line of the railway is now part of the cycle path between Bathgate and Seafield.

In the 1960s, when peat mosses were still perceived as waste ground, Easter Inch Moss was considered a problem. West Lothian county council acquired it with the intention of reclaiming the land and using it to provide leisure facilities for the New Town of Blackburn. Proposals for the site included a golf course, sports pitches, and an artificial ski slope on Seafield Bing! Efforts were made to drain it under the guidance of Anders Tomter, an international expert in peat moss reclamation. However, drainage of peat mosses must be constantly maintained: at Easter Inch this work was neglected, the pipes became warped and clogged, and the area reverted to bog.

Since then, attitudes have changed, and peat mosses are now valued and conserved as unique habitats supporting a range of plant and animal life. West Lothian council is seeking designation of Easter Inch Moss as a Local Nature

Reserve, to exploit it as an educational resource on the environment. Seafield Bing, now renamed Seafield Law, has been contoured and relandscaped to resemble a natural hill.

Agriculture

With the selling off by Thomas Douglas of much of the Blackburn estate, Blackburn became an area of farming owner-occupiers. Farming was still of sufficient importance in the 1860s to support a Blackburn Ploughing Society, which held annual ploughing competitions. However, with the disturbance of the underground drainage by coal mining, especially at the west end of Blackburn, much farmland was degraded, and today the farms are mostly dairy. In 1994, the Redhouse Farm

Peggy Galloway collecting milk from Blackburn farms, with her horse, Danny, 1920s and 1930s.
Russell Hannah

dairy was the source of an outbreak of e-coli food poisoning, which resulted in the tragic death of a young child.

In 1935, Blackburnhall Farm was acquired by the Department of Agriculture for Scotland, and divided up into ten smallholdings. The government's small-holdings scheme was intended to address the problem of de-population of the countryside, as well as overcome the social isolation that made many young people leave farm work. The smallholdings at Blackburnhall were used for a variety of purposes – market gardening, pig rearing and poultry keeping – and survived until the 1970s. The holdings have been sold and nowadays some are used as purely residential homes; but the rural businesses which flourish today include a car repair workshop and a livery stable.

British Leyland

British Leyland Truck and Tractor Plant, Bathgate, in the 1970s.
West Lothian Council Libraries

The Conservative government of Harold Macmillan noted the slow decline of heavy industries and put pressure on several major industries to set up in areas suffering the loss of mining or heavy manufacturing jobs. In 1960, the British Motor Corporation was persuaded to build its new truck and tractor plant on a site between Bathgate and Blackburn. There was jubilation at the prospect of 6,000 jobs to replace those being lost in the moribund shale industry and the contracting coal industry; but there was trepidation among the local authorities at the extent of development that would be necessary. The local workforce could not fill all the new jobs, and many thousands of incomers to the area would have to be housed.

The first sod of the new factory was cut in June 1960, and in October 1961 the first truck rolled off the assembly line. In the 1960s and 1970s, the BMC flourished and expanded. Trouble, however, was in store. Money which should have been invested in the Bathgate plant was diverted to the ailing car division in England. The ancillary industries which were supposed to follow BMC (which became British Leyland in 1968) stayed in the south. The market was highly competitive, the national economy was in recession, and Leyland's market share was overtaken by Ford in 1977. To add to the company's troubles, this was a time of trade union militancy and the plant was hit by a series of official and unofficial strikes. The company retaliated by withdrawing some planned investment, and labour relations went from bad to worse with a breakdown of trust between men and management. In the late 1970s and early 1980s, the range of models built at Bathgate was reduced; by 1984 only two were in production and the 6,000 workforce had been reduced to 2,000. A staggered closure was announced that same year, and the gates finally closed in 1986.

Despite its unhappy ending, BMC and British Leyland helped West Lothian through a very difficult period, giving employment to thousands, and bringing new life to the area. The jobs in the offices and canteens were significant to women's employment, and despite the large influx of newcomers, there were plenty of jobs to go round, so preventing some of the resentment that might otherwise have been felt. 'Local people' said one Blackburn man, 'were just happy to see their sons get out of the pits.'

Whitehill Industrial Estate and Some Local Firms

In 1960, 29 acres of land on Whitehill Farm were acquired by West Lothian County Council and earmarked for industrial use. The intention was to provide employment for those whose skills (or lack of them) made them unsuitable for BMC. The council realised that BMC could not solve all the local unemployment, especially among women. In 1964, the site was extended to cover some 150 acres,

Russell of Bathgate factory in 1962.
West Lothian Council Libraries

which, the council hoped, would support 15–20 factories and provide some 5,000 jobs. It was expected that the 'spin-off' industries following BMC to Bathgate would take up the sites. Other than the two small estates at Broxburn, Whitehill was the first major industrial estate to be established in West Lothian. The first sites were ready by 1965. To entice industry, an 'Estate Centre' was planned, with shops, bank, restaurant, clubs, bus station, administrative office and weighbridge, but this ambitious scheme came to nothing.

In 1981, a local authority report judged that Whitehill was 'noticeably unsuccessful and provides few jobs.' The ancillary firms had failed to follow Leyland to Bathgate, and the estate was unable to compete with the more attractive incentives on offer in Livingston New Town. Since then, occupancy has risen, and Whitehill is now flourishing. There is some owner occupation and a public private partnership has seen the development of a business centre at the entry to the estate. The largest employers are United Central Bakeries Ltd., MRS Distribution Ltd., and Dana Glacier Vandervell Ltd., manufacturers of bearings for private and commercial vehicle engines.

A smaller industrial enterprise was set up in 1978, when ten 'nest units' for small businesses were set up on the land across the road from St Kentigern's Academy. This was agreed to despite the opposition of Blackburn's Councillor Angus

McGillvery, who said, perhaps not very helpfully, that 'Blackburn has been a mess, still is a mess and to add this to it would certainly not make it any more pretty.'

One home-grown firm which has been a notable success is Matt Purdie and Sons. The business was begun in 1960 as a coal delivery firm in Livingston Station, moved to Blackburn, and expanded into removals and, more recently, storage. The coal merchant's business has been given up, but the firm prospers, employing 22 people on the site that was once the Mill of Blackburn.

Another successful local firm was Russell of Bathgate, hauliers, warehouse and distribution contractors. This business was started in West Calder in 1939 with just two lorries, and expanded into a large firm with depots in Bo'ness, Leith, Glasgow and London. An offshoot of this firm was the Central Garage in Bathgate Road; the large depot and head office, also in Bathgate Road, opened in 1961 (and is now home to Wincanton Logistics). The garage closed in 1975, and the haulage firm closed in 1984 with the loss of 60 jobs.

CHAPTER 14

Shops and Pubs

BLACKBURN HAS HAD MARKETS and fairs since at least 1696, when the Scottish Parliament granted to Patrick Murray of Livingston (who also owned the Barony of Blackburn) the right to hold three yearly fairs (the first Tuesdays of June and August and the last Thursday of October) and a weekly market on Thursdays in Blackburn.

Blackburn fairs continued into the 18th and 19th centuries, but came to be more for games, sports and entertainment than for the sale of produce. The people of Blackburn were within walking distance of Bathgate, with its shops, markets and fairs.

The old fermtoun of Blackburn had no shops; craftsmen made the few goods that were required, so there was no need for shop premises. As prosperity grew in the 1800s, shops began to appear in Blackburn, and the shopkeeper began to intervene between the producer of goods and the purchaser, to the convenience of all sides. The capital required to set up a shop was modest. The business could be run from the home, and there were no environmental health or bureaucratic regulations to worry about.

The earliest trade directory for Blackburn dates from 1825–26, at which time Blackburn had two grocers and spirit dealers (John Glasgow and David Shanks) and one woollen draper and grocer (John Turnbull). Blackburn, with its large cotton mill and canvas factory, was described as 'a thriving little place,' yet it appears to have had no shops other than the three mentioned above.

By 1837, there were several grocers in Blackburn, as well as a baker and two shoemakers. By 1852, there were six grocers, two tailors, one baker, and no less than four shoemakers. Fifteen years later, in 1867, the shoemakers had all gone, but two drapers were in business, and six grocers, of whom two also sold spirits.

It would be a mistake to think of these shops in any way resembling modern shops with their plate glass windows and enticing displays of goods. Early shops were merely a room of a dwelling house – sometimes a room in which the family also lived. Plate glass windows did not become common until the 1880s and 1890s and the early shops would have been small, dark, and limited in the range of unpackaged goods on sale.

The Company Store

William Kelly would have been familiar with the company store at the New Lanark Mills, and in all probability set up a store for his employees at the Blackburn Cotton Mill. Most large companies, especially the coal companies, found it profitable to set up a company store. Some obliged their workers to shop there; in the worst cases, part of the wages was paid in tokens for the store. These 'truck shops' were notorious for poor quality, short measures and high prices. Workers could very easily get into debt to the store, and debt put them in thrall to their employers. The government passed many acts against the truck system, but it proved hard to abolish, being so profitable to the companies. It's not known whether the Blackburn Cotton Mill store was a truck shop. It may not even have been strictly a company store, merely some company premises let to a shopkeeper and run for his own profit. There was certainly a store in Cotton Mill property in the 1860s, kept by shopkeeper John Thomson, and he was still there at the time of the fire in 1877.

Increasing prosperity brought new kinds of businesses selling 'luxury' items rather than necessities. Off-the-peg clothes came within reach of the purses of ordinary people from the 1860s, when drapers became common. A confectioner's shop was set up in the 1880s, a newsagent in the 1890s, and the first hairdresser and barber about 1910 – 'Anthony Constance, Blackburn Shaving Saloon: 100 Private Pots are in stock for any Customer wishing to have his own private Brush and Pot.' Three generations of Constances were Blackburn's barbers. By 1914, Blackburn had its own photographer, James Philip, whose unique selling point was: 'Football and other grounds Photographed.' William and Alexander Forsyth were coach-hirers, grocers, drapers, spirit dealers, egg merchants, seedsmen and iron-mongers, and flourished from the 1880s. William Forsyth was also Inspector of the Poor, clerk to the parish council, Collector of Rates, and clerk to Livingston parish school board – truly a man of many talents. More recent businesses may still be remembered by older residents: David Young the baker; the three confectioner's shops, Liddell's, Smith's and Galloway's; Young's the newsagents; and Foyd Ezzi's sweet shop – 'yellow ice-cream, second to none.'

From about 1850 to 1920, the village was served by some twelve to fifteen businesses, i.e. shops and pubs. With the new council housing, the number of shops expanded until, in 1958, the village was served by some 25 shops, seven pubs, hotels and cafes, a bank, two filling stations and a police station. In the days before widespread car ownership, when shopping had to be done locally, all the essentials could be bought in Blackburn. These shops were supplemented by a number of mobile shops: Jim Walker recalls an 'array of tradesmen in grocery, butcher, fish and baker vans who visited the street regularly, announcing their arrival with beeping vehicle horns or in stentorian voices, verbally advertising their wares. Most things could be purchased on a daily basis without ever leaving the house, which was good news because household refrigerators were virtually non-existent. Perishables therefore were bought as and when required.'

The Shopping Centre

After the Second World War, Blackburn continued to grow with the expansion of council housing in the village. The shops were still concentrated along Main Street, so there was a need for shops nearer the new housing to the north. The council built some shop units in the Riddochhill Scheme. Each came with a house for the shopkeeper – an inducement to traders to come to the area. The Hopefield Drive shops opened in 1956 and continue to trade today.

By 1961, the council's plans for the expansion of Blackburn were well advanced, and a new town centre was planned – shops, a supermarket, hotel, civic centre and public library. The intention was to replace the existing shops in the Main Street with a new shopping centre of 43 units in typical 1960s style – concrete, open air, but with a covered way to keep shoppers dry. The units were quickly let, and the Centre opened in 1966. Hays, a large supermarket chain, opened a supermarket in September 1966, under the management of George Douglas, who had learned his trade in the Blackburn branch of West Calder Co-op.

The new shopping centre was expected to end Blackburn's traditional dependence on Bathgate, but a writer in the *West Lothian Courier* perceptively pointed out that every Saturday many hundreds of housewives from all the local villages came to Bathgate to shop, even though they could get all that they wanted at home. 'Since time immemorial the housewife has made the weekly shopping trip an occasion, a break from the daily routine. That is the attraction just as much as the shops...'

Within five years of the opening of the shopping centre, the population began to fall. Too large for the town, the shopping centre soon suffered from the air of neglect caused by empty units. Vandalism was always a problem, as were gangs of youths hanging about in the evenings. Concrete buildings, unless well maintained, soon begin to look neglected. The private owners of the shopping centre failed to maintain it, and by the late 1980s it was in a poor state.

The proximity of Bathgate, with its wide range of shops, hindered Blackburn's establishing itself as a shopping centre. By the 1960s, even Bathgate was being challenged by other centres as a result of the greater ease of travel by public transport

Blackburn Shopping Centre in decay, 1998. The covered ways acted as funnels for swirling winds and litter.
Helen Scott

and increasing car ownership. The growth of Livingston as a shopping centre since the 1970s has absorbed even the market for everyday items. The number of shops in Blackburn fell to an absolute minimum in the late 1990s, and the difficulties Blackburn shop-keepers faced in competing with major retailers was compounded by the dreadful condition of the shopping centre in Blackburn.

The Mill Centre, 2002.
West Lothian Council Libraries

It took years of pressure by shopkeepers, community council and West Lothian Council before the owners, Trendgrove, agreed to sell and the shopping centre could be upgraded. The substantial rebuilding was carried out while the existing shops continued to trade. The centre was enclosed, and the shop units reduced to twelve, plus the Scotmid store and a Council Information Services office. The old name of Sycamore Walk was abandoned, and in 1999 a new name was given – the Mill Centre – suggested by Lesley Marr (7) of Blackburn Primary School to recall the Cotton Mill and the textile heritage of Blackburn.

The Co-operative

The Co-operative movement was an extraordinary phenomenon in the 19th and 20th centuries. Part of the self-help movement within the working class, and formed at least partly in response to the truck system, it began with a vision of a time when 'men and women would be free to spend their hard-earned wages to the fullest possible advantage in a business controlled and managed by themselves.' Profits were divided among the membership according to how much each had spent. The more you spent, the more you saved in the form of the dividend. The Co-op provided a simple way for working people on low wages to build up their savings. The highest dividend ever paid in the local area was four shillings in the pound, by West Calder Co-operative in 1902. Critics claimed that high dividends were achieved by overcharging, but the high level of membership over a long period of time suggests that most customers were satisfied.

Small co-operative societies were started all over West Lothian – e.g. Uphall, Gavieside, Oakbank – but some were too small to be viable and were wound up or taken over by the larger societies. The most successful of all was West Calder Co-operative, founded in 1875, which had the distinction of being from the first wholly run by working men – miners and oil workers – without any interference from the oil or coal companies.

Blackburn branch of West Calder Co-operative Society, East Main Street.
West Lothian Council Libraries

Collision

In 1887 a West Calder Co-operative horse-drawn van collided with a pony trap, whose two passengers were seriously injured. One was John Wallace, inspector of the poor at Blackburn, and the other was a Blackburn shopkeeper, William Marshall. Payment for the damage to the trap was under discussion when Mr Wallace's condition deteriorated and he died. His widow then brought a legal action against the West Calder Society for £5,000 damages. Rumours flew about the district that the Society would be ruined, and some members rushed to withdraw their cash. Prompt payment of all these claims restored confidence and checked the run on the Society's capital.

After a prolonged enquiry and a trial which appeared to hinge on the temperaments of the two horses involved in the collision, damages of £900 were awarded against the Society, reduced on appeal to £500. The Society weathered the storm and was not deterred from opening a branch in Blackburn a few years later.

The success of the West Calder Society in its home village encouraged it to extend its services to surrounding villages. At first a van service from West Calder served Blackburn, but in 1891 a building was bought and a branch opened. Business was so brisk that new premises were acquired close to the Crown Inn.

The Co-op gala day, 1923. Left to right: Annie Graham, Mr Duncan, Cissie Meek, Mrs Duncan, Jocky Rankine, Nellie Meek

Violet Carson

When the branch first opened in 1891, the membership was 100. By 1925, the membership had risen to 659, a third of the total population of Blackburn, and sales had reached a total of £35,000. Each member therefore was spending an average of £1 per week in the Co-op – a large part of a family's income when the weekly wage might be no more than £2 or £3.

The Co-op was more than just a shop; it was a way of life. Social functions were held for the benefits of members – outings, parties and dances, and gala days for the children. Classes in cookery, sick nursing and other topics were held. Experience gained in Co-operative committee work led many office bearers into local or national politics.

Gala Day

'The West Calder Co-operative Society (Blackburn Branch) held their annual gala in the Haugh Park. The children to the number of 600 met at the Infant School, and, headed by West Calder Public Band, paraded the streets which were beflagged for the occasion. After entering the field, the children were supplied with cakes, sweets and milk.'

The Blackburn Co-op continued to operate from its East Main Street store under manager John Burt between the wars; and after the second war, under managers who included Johnny Aitken (who sported an eye patch), Henry McCormack, and Alfred Dunlop. In the 1960s, the county council intended to expand Blackburn into a substantial town of some 10,000 people, and the Co-op prepared for the expected growth by building a supermarket on the site of the old Murrayfield farmhouse and steadings. The store was opened in December 1965 by local MP, Tam Dalyell and his wife Kathleen, and was the largest supermarket in West Lothian, at least twice as large as any then in Bathgate. It was completely different from the old type of store – self-service, no membership, no Co-op number to remember, and no dividend. The new shop was the first to be run by a partnership between the Scottish Co-operative Wholesale Society and the retail Co-operative Societies – in this case, Bathgate and West Calder. It was the first shop to open in the new Blackburn shopping centre, and sold 'everything except furniture.'

Despite all the difficulties when Blackburn failed to grow to its expected size and the shopping centre became sadly run down, the Co-op (now trading as Scotmid) remained faithful to Blackburn, and Blackburn shoppers to the Co-op. When the Mill Centre was rebuilt, Scotmid too was refurbished, and it continues to trade, the anchor store for the Mill Centre, and an essential facility, especially for elderly people and those without cars.

The Post Office

In 1834, a number of the leading inhabitants of Blackburn petitioned for the setting up of a post office in the village.

> Blackburn, 2 July 1834
>
> Dear Sir,
> We a few of the Principal inhabitants of Blackburn and Neighbourhood have long felt it a sore grievance the want of a Post Office in this Village, which contains about seven hundred inhabitants, besides two Large Factories, one in the Cotton and the other in the Flax lines ... and the Village is still extending in Building every year and also in manufactories, having no Post Office nearer than three miles distant.

Those who signed the letter included many connected with the mills and shops of Blackburn whose businesses were hampered by the lack of a post office. The petition was granted and a post office was set up in October 1834. It came under the Whitburn post office, the post being stamped with the Whitburn post mark, until about 1852, when a Blackburn mark was first used. A postman brought the mail every day from Bathgate to Whitburn, and on to Blackburn, and then made the same journey in reverse. During the first year a small loss was incurred, but as Post Office officials realised that Blackburn was a 'thriving village,' they anticipated that revenues would increase.

So Blackburn got and kept its post office. The first postmaster was a woman, Christian Dymock, who kept the job until the 1850s, when it was transferred to her husband, William Prentice. The post office was on the south side of the Main Street, at the head of the Rat Road, conveniently situated for the Cotton Mill, which would have been the biggest user of the postal service. At this time, the post office was set up in the premises of whoever was appointed postmaster, so its location changed frequently. After the opening of the new shopping centre at Sycamore Walk, the post office moved there, and it continues to operate from the new Mill Centre.

Public Houses

In 1828, the earliest year for which ale licences survive, there were four licensees in Blackburn – John Dougall, Erskine Gray, James Orr and John Turnbull. That is not to say that there were four pubs in the village, only that four householders had the right to sell ale. In fact, there seems to have been no inn in Blackburn at that time. John Turnbull had a drapery and licensed grocer's shop; the other three probably sold ale from their own homes. Another early licensee was a woman, Christian Waterstone, who held an ale licence from at least the mid 1830s.

The first person in Blackburn to be termed an innkeeper was James Dougal in 1860, though he had held an ale licence since 1847. His inn was probably the Almond. Its next licensee was another woman, Christian Leishman. By 1868, John Carlaw, son of the Blackburn grocer, James Carlaw, was the innkeeper of the Almond, and he remained there till 1900. The present Almond Inn was built about 1898. The pub's best-known licensee was probably Robert Savage, whose wife was a teacher at Redhouse School.

The Crown Inn, c.1910.
West Lothian Council Libraries

The Crown Inn opened in the late 1860s, and was owned by Mrs Agnes Sayer, widow of the owner of the Hopefield Mill. A more recent publican was Kenny Campbell, who during his army service was batman to George Younger, a member of the Younger's beer dynasty, and later a Secretary of State for Scotland. Kenny is said to have saved George Younger from some dangerous incident, and in return was given his tenancy. Blackburn's 'characters,' especially those of the mining fraternity, met in the Crown Inn, whose light ale was famous. It was very much a man's pub – 'We don't serve cocktails and we don't serve women.'

The Turf is the youngest of Blackburn's three pubs, and was opened in 1899 by Thomas Wallace, already the owner of the Market Inn in Mid Calder and the Almond Inn in Blackburn. It was the first of Blackburn's pubs to be bought by a commercial company – the Commercial Brewery in Edinburgh – about 1936. That same year, Dr Buck Ruxton of Lancaster was hanged for the murder of his wife and his housemaid, Mary Jane Rogerson. Mary is said to have been a barmaid at the Turf before going into domestic service.

The three pubs established in Victorian times continue to flourish today. They have always been centres of Blackburn's social life, originally for men only, but now to a lesser extent for women too. They continue to support various teams – pool, darts, dominoes, even football – and are an important means of informal socialising in these less sociable times. New licensed premises were opened in the 1960s and 1970s, but they have not proved such good survivors. Provided for the increased population of the 1960s and 1970s, most of them declined along with the population in the 1980s.

In 1954, William Connolly opened a grocer's shop at the foot of Mill Road, and his County Tavern public house opened next door the following year. Willie Connolly and James Boyle (best known as county councillors) were also the owners of the County Printers. Willie Connolly was the last county convener of West Lothian county council, and the first of the new district council. In the early 1970s, when the council planned a new main road through Blackburn, several properties on the north side of West Main Street were purchased for demolition. The County Tavern was among the properties knocked down, but the road was never built.

The New Blackburn Athletic Social Club began on West Main Street, opposite the County Tavern, then, as membership increased, ground was bought in Riddochhill Road and a social club built, complete with function room, lounge, and games room. The social club was intended to provide financial security for the football club, but it was just one of several licensed clubs in Blackburn competing for shrinking custom. It closed in 1978, reopening later as the Ladeside Inn. By 1993, the Ladeside was suffering from neglect; electrical faults made it a considerable danger and the council's environmental health officers had it closed down.

The Golden Hind opened in 1967. Owned by Tennent Caledonian, its function room upstairs was a popular choice for weddings and dances, but its fortunes declined with those of the shopping centre. A brief attempt in 1991 by the new owners, John Ward and Derek Wilson, to modernise the pub and attract more

The Golden Hind Hotel straddled the shopping centre – 'a striking example of contemporary architecture and simulates the effect of a ship'.

Jean Fooks

customers, with entertainments, karaoke and bands, was doomed to failure, as the whole of the Sycamore Walk area deteriorated. The Hind closed down about 1992, then lay empty and dilapidated for several years, abused by squatters and vandals. It was eventually demolished when the old shopping centre was replaced in 1999.

The Golden Circle Hotel was opened by Usher Vaux in 1964 to serve the business market brought by BMC, and its strikingly modern tower made it a landmark in the district. Thanks to a well-established line in weddings and other functions, and the proximity of Livingston New Town, it managed to survive the closure of British Leyland. Its tower and outward appearance were modified in 1998 when it reopened as the Cairn Hotel, part of the MacDonald Hotels group.

Other Blackburn pubs came and went – the Grand Prix, Rico's, and Chadwick's (in the former Co-op premises). The Jolly Roger proved more durable and continues as the Happy Valley in Bathgate Road.

The British Leyland Social Club

The British Leyland Social Club opened at Christmas 1971; the culmination of many years of planning. Almost from the time BMC came to Bathgate, employees had contributed 6d per week from their wages. The club opened on land near the motorway, but with an entrance off Beechwood Road that was not easy to find. In keeping with the size of the Leyland factory, this was a huge club with a games room, lounge, meeting rooms and a function hall that could hold up to 1,000. In its heyday, it had between 5,000 and 6,000 members, top acts came to perform, and there were three bars and some twenty bar staff. But as the number of men employed at Leyland declined, so did the club, and these difficulties were compounded by the general loss of popularity of social clubs in the late 1970s. Membership declined to 3,500 and the club moved into the red. Despite strenuous efforts to save it, the club called in the liquidators in late 1981, exactly ten years after it opened.

CHAPTER 15

Housing before the New Town

THE EARLIEST HOUSES IN the New Town of Blackburn were thatched cottages, each opening onto the street at the front, but with a small strip of ground at the back for growing vegetables or keeping a few hens or a cow. These houses were built by the householders for their own use. The more prosperous might also build or buy a property and rent it out in order to produce a little income. Neither George Moncrieff nor his successors built any houses for rental to their villagers.

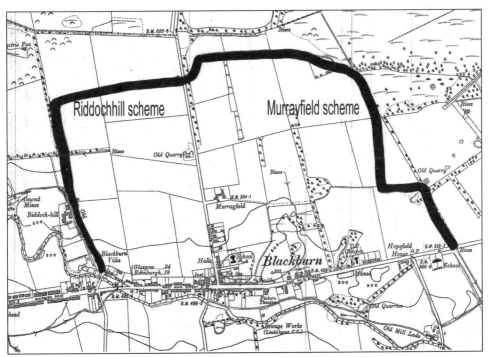

Old Blackburn, compared with Blackburn today. The dark line shows the present extent.
Ordnance Survey

The Cotton Mill owners required such a large workforce that they had to build some houses to attract workers to the village. By the time of the fire in 1877, Robert Gilkison & Co. owned 35 houses in the village. The row of cottages at the west end of the village, just east of the bridge and on the south side of the

Main Street, may be survivors of the mill-workers' housing. These, and some of the houses in the old Rat Road are probably the oldest in the village, built in the late 18th or early 19th centuries.

The Ordnance Survey mapmakers of the mid 1850s noted that Blackburn's houses were a mix of one and two-storey, with gardens behind, and generally in good repair. As the population continued to grow in the 19th century, house building barely kept pace. For most of the Victorian era, Blackburn's houses, mostly room and kitchen, were by modern standards grossly overcrowded. On the other hand, they were no more overcrowded that those in the other towns and villages of West Lothian at the time. Local authorities had no powers to raise money to spend on house building. Private employers only built company houses when they needed to attract workers. There was no incentive for anyone – private individual, speculative builder or large employer – to build *good* housing. On the low wages of the time, few could afford to pay the higher rent for a better standard of housing.

George Terrace, housing for Whitrigg miners. In the distance are Redheugh houses, originally Paul's Buildings, for Riddochhill miners. Now the site of St Kentigern's Academy.
West Lothian Council Libraries

Towards the end of the 19th century and in the early years of the 20th century, the last of the old thatched cottages gave way to two-storey tenements, each housing several families. Some of them survive in Main Street to this day. Residents of the older cottages still had to bring all their water from a street well, and use outside privies at the back, shared by several families. In 1895, the council discussed an outbreak of typhoid in Blackburn believed to be caused by sewage from the privies running into the public well at Albert Buildings next to the Crown. During the discussion, Dr Kirk declared that Blackburn was in 'a frightful state' (sanitarily speaking). Shortly after this, piped water was introduced, and newer houses were generally built with an inside WC and water supply. Nevertheless, in 1901, West Lothian was the worst-housed county in Scotland.

As the workforce of the local coal mines grew, the mining companies were obliged to provide housing as a means of attracting miners to their employ. In 1909, Riddochhill Colliery's owners, Gavin Paul & Sons, built twenty single-storey houses at the west end of the village, on the north side of the road; twelve were two-roomed, four three-roomed and four were single ends. The houses included indoor WC and scullery, with gardens to the rear, and were considered good of their kind. These were known as Paul's Buildings; when Gavin Paul sold out to Baird's, they were renamed Redheugh Houses.

In 1913, Whitrigg's owners, Forrester & Company, were building some 50 houses, also at the west end. On the north side were twenty three-apartment houses, and on the south side, 34 two-apartment houses. In honour of the then King and Queen, the houses were named George Terrace (north side) and May Terrace (south side). More houses were built to the east of May Terrace at Mosshall Place, as well as new blocks behind Mosshall Place and May Terrace, making a total of some 80 Whitrigg houses in Blackburn. By then, Blackburn was suffering from ribbon development: it had become a narrow village stretching along the Main Street for over a mile.

Despite these new houses, the housing problem in Blackburn was becoming more serious because of the village's growing population. The shortage of houses was made worse by the large number of houses which fell below adequate standards – low as these standards were in the early twentieth century. In 1919, West Lothian county council's Sanitary Inspector for the Bathgate district produced a detailed report on housing needs. Of Blackburn, he reported that no less than 70 houses (almost one in five) were substandard and should be demolished. In addition, a further 30 new houses were needed. At this time, Blackburn had 360 houses, of which some 135 were coal company houses. All the others were privately owned or rented. With a population of 1,903, this meant an average of five persons per household, most of them in two-roomed accommodation – seriously overcrowded by modern standards. But as councillors realised, there was no point in turning people out of overcrowded houses if there were no other houses for them to go to.

With such a desperate need for more houses, it might be wondered why private builders did not rush to fill the market. But few people had the money to buy outright. The demand was for rented accommodation, and, for a small builder, this was too slow and uncertain a return on a large outlay of money. So, over the years, private enterprise failed to provide enough houses, and the large mining companies failed to provide *good* enough houses.

This long-standing problem, which was repeated to some degree throughout industrial central Scotland, could only be tackled with government help. At last, in 1919, the government passed the Housing, Town Planning (Scotland) Act (better known as the Addison Act), which *obliged* local councils to make provision for decent housing and offered subsidies to finance their house building.

Development to the south of Blackburn has always been hindered by the River Almond, so the village had to be developed to the north of the Main Street. A start was made quickly, when the county council entered negotiations with the Torbanehill estate to buy a field to the west of the Bathgate road. Matters were then allowed to lapse, until in June 1924, councillors were asked to 'report what they considered to be the number of houses immediately required in their various districts.' With this casual approach, the Blackburn councillor came up with the figure of from 150 to 200 houses, which by 1925 had been reduced to 100; and by the time building began, to 52.

By 1926, thirteen blocks of houses of the four-in-a-block type were under construction. Thirty-two were two-apartment houses and twenty were three-apartment, and the first tenants moved in during 1927. At a meeting in 1929, the district committee decided to call the two new developments Murrayfield Crescent and Edgar Crescent; but no more was heard of these names and the addresses reverted to Bathgate Road.

Despite the prevalence of large families, the three-apartment houses proved slower to let, presumably because of the higher rents. When the next scheme of house building was being prepared, the council wished to build mostly two-apartment houses. However the Board of Health stipulated that the larger proportion should be three-apartment houses – fortunately, for future Blackburn residents. By the 1930s, rents had come down, and the average annual rent of a two-apartment was £14 and of a three-apartment, £17.

In 1932, the government subsidy for council housing was cut by a third, and it was discontinued altogether in 1935. Instead subsidies were made available for 'slum clearance' and for the housing which replaced it. No money was available for the repair of old properties, only for demolition and replacement, and as a result some interesting old properties in Blackburn were lost. It was reported to the County Council Housing Committee that 'the dwelling houses known as the Barracks, occupied by persons of the working classes, are unfit for human habitation' and they were partly demolished in 1934; and in 1935, Dook Raw was knocked down. Some 48 houses, designed and laid out by Matthew Steele, a highly regarded Bo'ness architect, were decided upon in 1934; a further 96 were built under the 1935 Housing Act, and still more were planned or under construction when the war intervened.

By the outbreak of the Second World War in 1939, 240 council houses had been completed in Blackburn – on Bathgate Road, and Riddochhill Road, Crescent and Drive. During the war, practically all house building came to a halt, but despite shortages of materials and workmen, it resumed soon after hostilities came to an end. The Scottish Special Housing Association, a quasi-governmental agency set up in 1937 with the remit of building working class housing in the 'Special Areas' (suffering from the decline of the heavy industries), also undertook a major programme of house-building in West Lothian, and started building in Blackburn after the war.

In the fifteen years after 1945, driven by the increase of population coming to jobs in the local mines, the county council built 350 houses in Blackburn, and the SSHA another 330. During this period, the first building took place on the east side of Bathgate Road – the SSHA houses in Mosside Drive, Road and Terrace; and the Riddochhill Scheme was fully developed: Hopefield Drive and Road, Ladeside Avenue, Drive and Road, Riddochhill Crescent, Drive and Road, Whitehill Drive, Road and View, and Yule Place and Terrace. The two last were named after Ninian Yule, who died in 1947.

Councillor Ninian Yule.
West Lothian Council Libraries

Obituary

'Mr Ninian Yule, chairman of the county council housing committee, died suddenly on Friday, aged 53. Mr Yule, who was an agent for the Co-operative Insurance Company, was cycling from Blackburn to Stoneyburn when he collapsed, and was removed to his home at 72 Riddochhill Road, Blackburn, where he died almost immediately. His passing removes one of our best known and most likeable public men. He became a member of the county council in 1932 and was appointed Convener of the Housing Committee in 1939. As such, he did a tremendous amount of hard work under very trying conditions, and that the county's housing programme has been carried through so far is due largely to his continuous oversight and drive... Many will miss his kindly, genial, unperturbable personality, and the helping hand he was always ready to give. Sympathy is expressed to his wife and two sons who survive him.'

George McCartney, and Sarah and Margaret O'Hagan outside 13 George Terrace in the 1920s. The houses were two up, two down. The living rooms had two box beds, and the stairs were so narrow that large upstairs furniture had to be brought in through the bedroom window. An inside WC was provided but no bathroom, so the old zinc bath had to be brought out on Saturday nights.

John McLaren

Among the houses in Ladeside Avenue were the prefabs; kit houses intended to solve the acute housing shortage after the war, and expected to last some ten years. The first families moved into these smart little two-bedroomed houses in 1946 and 1947. With their fitted kitchens, gas refrigerators, and metal fitted units in all the rooms, they were much loved by the families that grew up in them, and lasted twice as long as expected.

As new houses were being built, old substandard properties were removed. The coal company houses at the West End were taken over by the National Coal Board after nationalisation of the mines in 1947, and were gradually emptied. May Terrace and George Terrace, though considered good housing in their day, were unfit by modern standards of accommodation. The last mining company houses to survive were the original Riddochhill miners' cottages, Redheugh. They were finally removed in the 1960s, to make way for the building of St Kentigern's Academy. A great improvement came about in 1949, when electric power came to Blackburn, and the smelly gas mantles were no longer needed. Neil Mclauchlan, last of the Blackburn lamplighters, was made redundant. Electric light had been introduced by West Calder Co-operative Society as early as 1902, but seems initially to have lit just the store and possibly a few street lights nearby.

By the end of the 1950s, nearly 40 per cent of Blackburn's population was living in council or SSHA housing, which, though of reasonable standard, the council admitted was 'open and monotonous in appearance and could be improved by tree-planting...' The old part of the village was in poor condition and a number of houses were standing empty, awaiting demolition.

CHAPTER 16

A New Town Again

AS THE 1950S gave way to the 1960s, two factors were on the brink of changing Blackburn for ever: the Glasgow overspill and the British Motor Corporation's huge new factory.

Both these schemes were welcomed by West Lothian county council as a way of coping with the rising unemployment in the county. In 1959, the jobless total reached 2,306, the highest figure since before the war. The council's efforts to attract new industry to replace the jobs being lost in coal and shale mining seemed to have failed, so it decided to co-operate in a scheme being undertaken by Glasgow Corporation. Glasgow was notorious for its overcrowded tenements and was determined to clear the population from these houses so that they could be knocked down and the land redeveloped. Some 200,000 people were to be rehoused, an impossible task for Glasgow alone, so the Corporation approached other local authorities, asking them to take some of the 'overspill' population. To persuade these other councils, inducements were offered: government grants, a subsidy from Glasgow of £14 per year for each house, and, most importantly, the promise that industry would follow the relocated population.

So West Lothian county council decided that taking some Glasgow overspill was a way to bring both new people and new jobs to the area. In 1959, the council agreed to accept 300 Glasgow families, which meant over 1,000 people; and it undertook to 'provide and make available for letting Three Hundred new houses at Blackburn.' Blackburn was chosen because, although surrounded by coal mines, it was mainly free of under-mining and therefore the land was suitable for extensive house building.

So the overspill agreement was made in order to attract industrial development. But before the overspill families arrived, West Lothian discovered that it had been awarded the largest new industrial development in Scotland for many years. In 1960, the British Motor Corporation announced that it was to build its new truck and tractor factory at Bathgate. The company, it later emerged, was reluctant, but the Government was determined to disperse jobs to areas which were suffering from the decline of heavy industries.

Suddenly the council found it had a major problem. As well as houses for the 300 overspill families, it would need to provide houses for a large proportion of the 6,000 new workers at BMC. Bathgate, Whitburn and Armadale town councils would share the load, but the heaviest burden would fall on the county council. The county planning officer estimated that approximately 1,500 houses would have to be provided by the local authorities for BMC over the first three year period. The government would help with costs by giving an annual subsidy per house of £30. The council decided to take one community and build it up to cope with both the influxes. Blackburn, said councillor Willie Connolly, would become a new town and would more than double in population.

In 1960, the council acquired Murrayfield Farm for £16,197, and set to work. A scheme of five hundred houses was planned – 300 for the overspill families, and the others for tenants already on the housing list and some of the incoming BMC workers. The chosen site was on the east of Bathgate Road, north of the existing village. Another 66 houses were to be built on the west side, to complete the Riddochhill scheme. The population was expected to grow from 4,000 to 10,000 – nearly the same as Bathgate, and larger than Armadale or Whitburn.

Point blocks, Murrayfield, when brand new, 1960s.
West Lothian Council Libraries

To create a new town required more than just houses – a new shopping centre was to be built, and a new primary school, a restaurant, offices, and other facilities were also planned. To avoid total dependence on BMC, an industrial estate was to be created to provide jobs, particularly for women. Three hundred key workers at BMC were to be transferred from Birmingham, and it was expected that they would want to buy their own houses, so builders were to be invited to build 80–100 private houses in Blackburn.

The Glasgow overspill families were to be selected so that the main breadwinner's skills would be compatible with employment at BMC. Glasgow Corporation drew up a provisional list of tenants for acceptance by the county council. All the people on the list would be taking up industrial employment in West Lothian, and the council checked that the tenant had indeed been offered a job before approving his name. It was hoped to avoid creating a ghetto of Glasgow families by spreading them out throughout the town, to encourage integration with the existing population and with the other newcomers. In fact, all were put into the Murrayfield scheme, creating a very obvious physical division down the centre of the town – the old residents to the west of Bathgate Road, the new to the east. No one had asked the existing population of Blackburn if they wanted several hundred overspill families and there was some understandable resentment and apprehension, as Jim Walker recalls: 'Soon we would be overrun with strangers and not just any strangers but "Glesca keelies" with their wild ways and fondness for booze and violence.'

At a public meeting, Blackburn people had the chance to comment on the proposals. Foyd Ezzi, the newsagent and confectioner, pointed out that if all the shops were to be in a shopping centre off Bathgate Road then 'there would be little purpose in having a main street, and a village without a main street was like a dog without a tail.'

With the optimism of 1960s planners, the county planning officer, E.J. Hutton, promised that the houses would be 'modern buildings... and suitable to the 1960s, 70s and even 80s.' As well as building anew, the opportunity would be taken to clear away many of the old buildings in Main Street, some of which had become eyesores. The redevelopment did not include the area west of the bridge: as the NCB houses were emptied, they would be demolished. Blackburn was to become a larger town, but a more compact one.

The original plan approved by WLCC was amended by the Department of Health, which stipulated that the density of housing be increased from thirteen to twenty houses per acre: 90 bed spaces per acre, as opposed to 55 in the houses being built in the burghs of Whitburn, Bathgate, and Armadale. As a result, the plan was amended to include more blocks of flats and fewer terraced houses, a change that was to store up trouble for the future.

'Cottage Type, Please'

The application forms completed by overspill families and 'Incoming Industrial Workers' survive. One Glasgow family with six children aged between one and eleven was living in a two-room apartment in an abandoned property. It was not uncommon for a family of five or six to be living in a single end. One such applicant, who was living with his mother, wife and two children in a single roomed house, wrote: 'Owing to domestic troubles between my mother and wife, my wife and family are split, they are living at Forth and I have to live at Shotts so I can attend my work. No Traveling Convance' (sic). Each family was asked to specify the number of rooms they needed. Where a preference was stated, it was invariably for a house, not a flat: 'own door type preferred,' 'terrace type,' 'preferably not a flat, please,' '[we] desire very much a house with a back and front door, cottage type, please if possible consider this, as it's my dearest wish.' Meanwhile, the council was building 1,179 homes, 825 of them flats. From the start, they were building the type of home that people specifically did not want.

The architects were Messrs Alison, Hutchison and Partners, and the contractors were Crudens Ltd. of Musselburgh. The ground proved to be wet and peaty, so that piling was necessary to provide a firm foundation. Despite this, the houses went up quickly: work began in April 1961, the first ten houses were occupied by 30 October, and by October the following year, 500 house were completed, 350 were occupied, and piling operations for the next 500 had been begun. Lanarkshire Builders built another 80 flats in five-storey 'point blocks.'

Of the first phase, 300 were three-apartment, 175 were four-apartment, and 22 were five-apartment. No two-apartment houses were built – a great change from the assumption in the 1920s that only two-roomed houses were wanted. The first tenants were asked their opinion of the new houses: their reaction was mainly favourable but there were a few complaints: rainwater blowing under doors was a problem, as was the open plan layout without boundary fences, and flooding of the back greens – a portent perhaps of things to come.

Within ten years, things had gone sadly amiss for the New Town of Blackburn; within twenty years, Murrayfield had become a sink estate. What had gone so badly wrong? Three factors contributed to the deterioration of the Murrayfield estate: economic decline, social difficulties and architectural failings.

Economic Problems

Slab blocks, 1960s and 1980s.
West Lothian Council Libraries

Between 1961 and 1967, the county council built 1,179 houses in Blackburn –

5-storey point blocks	130	houses
5-storey slab blocks (deck access)	357	"
4-storey slab blocks (deck access)	236	"
3-storey flatted blocks	102	"
2-storey terraced cottages	333	" (the timbertops)
1-storey old people's houses	21	"

Total 1,179

Several hundred of the new houses were taken up by incoming BMC workers as the plant grew at the expected rate. However, in 1966-67, some 1,200 employees were made redundant, and many left the district to seek work elsewhere. Then the firm began to recruit again, and by 1970, 5,000 were employed. Blackburn's population rose to its highest ever figure in 1968 – over 9,000 – but once more economic factors caused British Leyland (as BMC had become in 1968) to lay off a considerable number of workers. And in 1968, Riddochhill Colliery closed down; hundreds of local men were made redundant, and many moved away in search of work. Between 1968 and 1971, the population of Blackburn dropped by over 1,300. In 1972, Whitrigg Colliery closed and another 635 jobs were lost to the local area. More miners left the area to seek work elsewhere. The number of empty houses in the Murrayfield estate rose to 370 in 1973, declined to 270 in late 1974, but rose again to nearly 400 in 1978, after further lay-offs at British Leyland. After a long decline, British Leyland finally closed down in 1986.

Compounding this problem of population loss was an oversupply of houses. The 1960s and 1970s were a period of extensive house building, not only in the county council areas, but also in Bathgate, Whitburn and Armadale burghs, and of course in Livingston, designated a New Town in 1962. With unemployment high, many people leaving the district to seek jobs elsewhere, and unemployed overspill families returning to Glasgow in search of work or at least the support of family and friends, fewer houses than expected were needed. Many of the new houses were standing empty. Tenants could afford to be choosy when deciding where to live, and most chose not to move into Murrayfield.

Social Problems

During the 1960s, Blackburn's population more than doubled – from 4,302 in 1961, to 9,051 (council estimate) in 1968. The early tenants suffered from a lack of community facilities, particularly shops. There was no council office in the village, so tenants perceived a lack of communication and consultation. The county council provided a range of facilities: by the early 1970s, the town had a shopping centre, two secondary schools, three primaries, a library, a community centre, and plenty of pubs, hotels and social clubs. But by the time social facilities were provided, the new tenants had got used to being without them, so they were little used. A council report recognised too late that 'When a new community is still on the drawing boards as at Blackburn... the incoming or existing population can very easily be made to feel outsiders, or antagonists in a municipal tenant-landlord situation. They ought to be made to feel that they share in the planned development. They also need to be made aware that the development is intended for them (and not, as sometimes appears to be the case, for the amour propre of the developing authority) and that their immediate needs are being understood and catered for.'

The Murrayfield scheme brought thousands of newcomers, most of them urban, into a small village, and this inevitably caused tensions on all sides. A small survey of Blackburn overspill families in 1966 found that one quarter of them were sorry that they had moved. The wives missed the closeness of tenement life, as well as the shops and the frequent bus services. Some families failed to settle, and moved back to Glasgow. Others liked their new life and their brand new houses, and found the local people friendly and welcoming. A *West Lothian Courier* writer in May 1963 visited the Ladies' Social Club, set up by Glasgow overspill families, whose membership within six months reached 112. The club was for incomers, but made determined efforts to meet with and entertain other clubs. Its members praised the help given them by the Miners' Welfare Committee, and said that what they missed most were the shops. 'It's all very well having vans, but you don't get the same variety. Most of the women travel into Bathgate on Friday mornings for their week's shopping. We're looking forward to the day when we have a shopping centre in Blackburn.' The article, intended to suggest that the newcomers were integrating with the existing population, in fact leaves the impression that the Glasgow overspill families were making their social life with other incoming families. However, the opposite view was put by Jocky Rankine: 'These folks may have come from Glasgow, but they belong to Blackburn now and are as much a part of it as those who were born here.'

The Murrayfield estate did not have the ideal social mix of tenants. The number of young families was far higher than average – 84 per cent of the overspill families had school-age children. The average household size in Murrayfield was 3.86 compared to the area average of 3.23, and 41 per cent of Murrayfield residents were under fifteen years of age, compared to 30 per cent in the rest of West Lothian. These children and young people did not always play in the areas provided for them. Their constant presence in common stairwells and access decks was a cause of annoyance, stress and even intimidation to some tenants. Empty houses attracted youngsters to hang about them, and incidents of fireraising and vandalism increased. A study of the problem in 1966 noted that 'this abnormally large age group will tend to elbow its way up through a society initially lacking the institutions to provide for it. It is essential that budding delinquency problems, even if they consist only of the noisiness and exuberance of an over-large teenage population, should be tackled at an early date by giving priority to the provision of recreational facilities for school children and adolescents.' Sensible words, but acted upon too late.

Unemployment or low wages also caused many social problems. Some of the Glasgow overspill families had been living in low-rent one or two-roomed houses and found it difficult to adjust to higher rents, lack of a family support system, and the need to furnish a larger house.

This is not to say that all the problem families were from the overspill. In fact the number of anti-social tenants was small, but one problem family was sometimes enough to empty a whole block of flats. As the environment and reputation of Murrayfield deteriorated, those who could do so moved away, and so the area was left with a higher than average number of 'problem' families. The tenants who wanted to take care of their properties and surroundings lost heart.

Unemployment sometimes led to debt, and inability to pay the bills. Former Blackburn resident Jim Walker recalls that because so many households had their electricity cut off, some flats were constantly in darkness, and were nicknamed 'the twilight zone.' Darkness and the appearance of being unoccupied encouraged vandalism. By 1978, several blocks contained only one or two tenants, and these semi-derelict blocks were a particular target of the vandals.

Architectural Problems

The estate was all-electric and the maisonettes had electric under-floor heating in the living room, hall and kitchen, but no heating at all in the bedrooms. The system was expensive to run; many tenants could not afford to heat their houses properly, and dampness and condensation soon set in. Flat roofs which leaked, poor insulation, plumbing and drainage systems, cheap materials and inadequate maintenance all compounded the problem.

The houses were built and landscaped in typical 1960s style – open plan layout with no fences or gardens. Washing was stolen from washing lines in unfenced back areas; the absence of front gardens created a lack of privacy; and instead of the open areas being perceived as everybody's space, the feeling was that they were nobody's, so nobody cared for them.

The 'slab blocks' were built with deck access, a popular style in the 1960s, intended to create communal 'streets' on each level. But they often became dumping grounds for rubbish, litter, even dog fouling; the presence of just one nuisance neighbour could scupper the efforts of all the other tenants to keep their deck decent.

The Murrayfield Blackburn General Improvements report of 1979 provides perhaps the best overall analysis:

> The need to provide accommodation quickly is, in a sense, at the root of the trouble. Blackburn was a small settled community gently sliding into old age when suddenly, in less than six years, its size was doubled by the building of a large estate quite unlike anything else in the village, and populated largely by newcomers. It was unrealistic to suppose that such a drastic event in the life of a small community would not cause problems, but just such an assumption (or hope) appears to have been made. Because housing was urgently required, a number of important things were done which would not normally have been done. The design process was truncated by the use of standard dwellings in standard blocks; the design problem was thus reduced to arranging the blocks on the site. A high density (relative to the rest of Blackburn) was adopted ... This speeded up the building process. Emphasis was placed on building houses, the community facilities being left until the completion of the housing programme. With the best possible motives, the council deferred to the requirements of BMC and left the community to look after themselves.

Trying To Fix It

As early as 1970, just three years after completion of the scheme, the county council admitted that Murrayfield was a problem. Over the next 15 years, a series of measures was introduced to try to reverse the trend, but it was merely tinkering with the problem. In 1973, the council commissioned the Architectural Research Unit (ARU) of Edinburgh University to produce a report and recommendations. Some improvements were carried out, but unless the whole estate could be turned around, Murrayfield's reputation would remain. As a council report said, 'people just do not want to live in Murrayfield.'

One lasting result of the University report was that it brought Tom Henney to Blackburn. The principal architect of the original report, he was so concerned

General view of Murrayfield estate, looking east, 1960s.
Aerofilms

with the problems and so impressed by the determination of the local residents to seek improvements, that when he was paid off by the council as consulting architect, he continued his involvement with Murrayfield for another 20 years – voluntarily and unpaid. His objective advice was a huge asset.

As a result of the recommendations of Tom Henney's report, a Residents' Association was formed and tenant participation was introduced into the planning process. The tenants' input and persistence over some twenty years was perhaps the most important factor in turning Murrayfield around. Alex Irvine, James McEwan, and the other members of Blackburn community council also played an active part in promoting the interests of their area, and fostering community involvement in the planning process, as did Councillor Willie Russell.

The ARU was asked to prepare three further reports suggesting solutions to the problems. Only the last of their reports was implemented: £170,000 was spent on 142 houses, spread over ten blocks. One of the cleared sites was sold for redevelopment as private housing, a surviving block was modernised for sale by a private developer, and the SSHA steel houses were upgraded and even won a Civic Trust commendation. But all these measures were merely scratching the surface of what had become a huge problem.

The two-tier system of local government introduced at regionalisation in 1975 caused further difficulties. Housing was a district responsibility, but social work lay with the region, and the district council sometimes felt that its efforts to persuade Lothian Region to invest in the Murrayfield estate were falling on deaf ears. Efforts had to be made to co-ordinate the work of the regional and district councils and to encourage public participation.

In 1976, Lothian regional council had identified Blackburn as an area of multiple deprivation. Unemployment was high and growing: by 1980 almost 1,000 further redundancies were expected at British Leyland, and its final closure was already feared. Murrayfield Primary School had the highest take-up of free school meals in West Lothian, and 20 per cent of its children came from one-parent families. Murrayfield produced three times as many social work referrals (many of them deriving from financial problems) as the rest of Blackburn, and Lothian Health Board identified Blackburn as one of six areas of special health needs in West Lothian, with a high incidence of child illness related to unhealthy housing conditions. With such melancholy distinctions, Blackburn earned inclusion in Lothian region's Urban Regeneration Programme.

In 1978, a more radical solution was proposed – extensive demolition. However, if houses were to be demolished, debts would remain for which there was no rent coming in, so both the tenants and the district council lobbied the Scottish Office to write off the outstanding capital debts on the Murrayfield estate. This was agreed to, and in 1979, 14 blocks of deck access maisonette flats were demolished.

There was no lack of will to get things right. In the mid 1980s, a dozen groups were operating in Blackburn – council, council-assisted and community groups: Blackburn Information Centre, Blackburn Initiatives Group, the Community Centre Management Committee, the community council, the Murrayfield Environmental Improvement Group (MEIG), Blackburn Youth Project, Blackburn Local Employment Scheme (BLES), the Community Block Association, the Young Families Support Project, the Community Information Centre, the West Side Action Group and the Blackburn Network. The very proliferation of groups may have resulted in duplication, and lack of liaison and co-operation except on an ad hoc basis. Many of the groups operated from the Community Block, a converted derelict block of flats which opened as community facilities and workshops in 1985 and was run by the Community Block Association, made up of representatives of the user groups.

Further improvements were undertaken. The eight 'point blocks' of flats were upgraded, the introduction of gas central heating being the single most important factor in making them more attractive to tenants. Three of the four-storey deck access blocks were reduced to two-storeys. But physical deterioration of the housing stock continued as the unemployment rate on the estate reached 48 per cent. In 1983 the district council set up a team of workers for Murrayfield, and for its other problem estate, Kirkhill in Broxburn. The teams were funded by the Urban Aid programme and were charged with looking at all aspects of the problem – physical, social, political and financial.

An extensive survey found that there was still a demand for the three-storey flats and point blocks – the timbertops even had a waiting list of eighteen months – but for the deck access blocks, there was no demand at all, in fact there were 261 empty properties – over a quarter of the total. However, the problems of leaking roofs in the timbertops persuaded MEIG to request that the council redirect its capital budget towards pitched roofs for the timbertops. The Urban Aid team concluded that despite the improvements already carried out, Murrayfield still needed a large injection of funding – at least £5 million, the equivalent of the district council's capital allocation for a whole year. But blue asbestos had been discovered on the Kirkhill estate, so the council's immediate attention turned to Broxburn. The needed millions were clearly not going to appear, unless central government stepped in.

A concerted campaign by MEIG bombarded the Scottish Office with letters and petitions. A video was made and sent to Michael Ancram, the Environment Minister. The response was not £5 million, but £250,000. It was a disappointment, but at least enabled the re-roofing of more of the timbertops, demolition of three point blocks in Rowan Drive, and upgrading of some semi-derelict houses.

In 1984, MEIG, which included representatives of the district council, Blackburn community council, the Urban Aid Team, Murrayfield tenants, and the independent adviser, Tom Henney, drew up a strategy; a five year plan showing year by year the problems that should be tackled. The main priorities were the demolition of the remaining five-storey deck access blocks; conversion of the four-storey deck access blocks to two-storey housing; re-roofing and re-cladding the remaining timbertops (where water penetration was becoming a major problem); and replacing the flat roofs of the three-storey flats with pitched roofs. Nearly £1 million was needed for each year of the work, and though in 1986 the district council agreed to the plan in principle, it was expected that the work would take much longer than five years.

In fact the work took not much longer than hoped for, and was managed gradually, without special help from central government. Guided by local people, the council gradually worked through the strategy. Instead of the horror stories of the 1970s, the *West Lothian Courier* in the late 1980s reported a series of achievements.

Renovated houses, Murrayfield, 1996.
Jean Fooks

John Miller, chairman of MEIG, boasted of Murrayfield becoming a desirable area: 'Who would have thought, even a couple of years ago, that anybody would pay £42,000 to live in Murrayfield – but that was the price of a private house which was sold here recently.' £200,000 was spent on re-roofing and constructing new fencing for 24 timbertop houses in Rowan Drive in 1990, and the last 44 were completed in the early 1990s. In 1992, Lord James Douglas-Hamilton, the Scottish housing minister, came to Blackburn to open the Horizon Housing Association development of 24 homes in Murrayfield, designed to suit wheelchair users.

A small park in Murrayfield was named after a founder member of MEIG,  John Liddell, who died in 1981. Another valued and long-serving committee member was Mary Wyper, secretary of MEIG from its founding. Sadly, Tom Henney did not live to see the full regeneration of Murrayfield, but his invaluable contribution has not been forgotten. Perhaps the debt might be acknowledged by naming some future housing development in his memory.

As well as improvements to housing, the landscape of the area was altered. Open plan landscaping gave way to private garden space and enclosed washing greens. Contained gardens for children were safer, and land was

Tom Henney
MEIG

better-kept when a pride of ownership was encouraged. Vandalism was reduced, and privacy increased. The success of the scheme was a long time coming, but that it came at last must be credited to the tenacity and persistence of the tenants themselves, particularly the members of MEIG, who never gave up trying, despite the years of disappointments and false hopes. Today Murrayfield is an attractive, low-rise estate, generally well-cared for, with an air of community pride. The houses are popular, and many have been bought by their tenants, showing a long-term commitment to and confidence in the future of Blackburn.

The private houses originally mentioned were slow in coming, and it was not until 1969 that Rattray Gardens, a development of four-roomed bungalows, was built. It was named by local builder Colin Drummond after his wife's home town of Rattray in Perthshire, and was the only private development in the whole town. In 1970, only 4 per cent of the housing stock was owner occupied; 96 per cent was local authority or SSHA stock – one of the highest figures in Scotland. Blackburn had become a community totally dependent on public housing, and it was a community with little social variation – 72 per cent were manual workers. The expectation that local authorities would provide housing for most of their residents was so firmly established by the 1970s, that it was scarcely questioned – until the political consensus was ended by the Thatcher government from 1979 onwards.

Conservative policy, not revoked by the succeeding Labour government, was to reduce the number of council houses and encourage instead provision by housing associations and by the private sector. Their 'right-to-buy' legislation has seen just over a third of Blackburn's council housing move from public to private ownership, and nearly three-quarters of the SSHA/Weslo housing stock. A number of builders have provided small developments of private houses, and gap sites have been filled by individuals building their own houses. There are still critics of the right-to-buy policy, and much can be said on both sides of the argument, but the popularity of council house sales in Blackburn suggests there has been an unmet demand for home ownership. The 2001 figures are 48 per cent public sector housing, and 47 per cent owner occupied. The change over the last 30 years is astounding. Blackburn still has some way to go to catch up with the level of owner occupation in West Lothian as a whole (63 per cent owner occupation and 32 per cent public rental), but the trend towards owner occupation is likely to continue.

There will always be council houses in Blackburn as long as there is a need for them, but in future they will only be for those unable to buy their own home. Despite all the mistakes and difficulties, Blackburn has cause to be grateful for local authority housing. It replaced the inadequate housing of the previous century and provided thousands of people with a decent home.

CHAPTER 17

Schools

A SCHOOL WAS PROVIDED in the parish of Livingston from at least the 17th century. It was open to all, though the fees would have deterred the poorest. This parish school, funded by the local heritors (land-owners) and under the supervision of the Church, was at Livingston Village; Blackburn was dependent on a 'private' school – run as a private business venture and funded solely by school fees. In 1760, Alexander Cuthbertson, the former coalmaster and poet, is referred to as the schoolmaster of Blackburn. The Old Statistical Account of the 1790s mentions that 'from 30 to 40 children are taught in a private school kept in the village of Blackburn.' This village school (now the Gospel Hall) had a 'leaky, mouldy, thatched roof and large plot of kitchen garden.' Its site had been granted free by the owner of Murrayfield Farm when the new village was being built in the late 18th century.

By the mid 1850s there were two subscription schools in Blackburn (paid for by subscriptions from parents and school fees). One of these was the village school. The other was a factory school, built by the owners of the Cotton Mill for their child workers and employees' children. Cotton mill employers were obliged to ensure that child employees attended school for half the week. From 1854, if these attendance levels were met, the government gave a donation towards the cost of running the school. In 1855 a grant of £5 was given to 'Blackburn School, R. Gilkison & Co.,' where fourteen half-timers from the Mill were at school. The Cotton Mill school, a modest single-storey building, could accommodate 100 children. The school-master was Mr Fife, whose salary was composed of school fees and £10 paid annually by the owners of the Cotton Mill.

Throughout the 1850s and 1860s, the village school had as its schoolmaster William Salmond, a Bathgate boy and a failed printer, who took up teaching in the days before professional qualifications were required. This school, being next door to the chapel of ease (see Chapter 18), was referred to as the Chapel School of Blackburn. It was in need of repair, and by 1860 a committee had been formed to raise subscriptions to build a new school, preferably at the west end, so that gas could be led in cheaply from the Cotton Mill. In 1867, the committee asked the parish heritors for financial assistance. The heritors answered that they had no legal right to use their funds for this purpose (being obliged only to support the one 'official' parish school in Livingston), but they recommended an appeal to the heritors as private individuals, 'as the object seems highly deserving.' A second approach was made by the Chapel School committee in 1868, but it received the same polite refusal. The title deeds of the school having been lost, there was difficulty in proving the community's ownership, and so the school's condition continued to deteriorate.

Children gather for the gala day outside the old Murrayfield school in Kidd Street, 1920s.
Janette Fowlds and Margaret Wilson

In 1872, education was taken over by the state, and was funded and supervised through an elected school board in each parish. Livingston school board built a new board school in Kidd Street. The old village school was substantially rebuilt and turned into a village public hall in 1877. Presumably the Cotton Mill school closed when the Mill burned down that same year.

The population of Blackburn continued to grow, however, and a large proportion of the inhabitants were children. The passing of the 1872 Education Act introduced compulsory attendance until the age of thirteen, with the result that school numbers increased. A new school was needed and in 1909, the Board of Education instructed the local school board to build one. A site was chosen at the extreme west end of the village, because the school was to serve the growing shale oil village of Seafield as well as Blackburn. Blackburn Public School (Redhouse) opened in October 1911, with accommodation for 300 pupils 'arranged in six class rooms for 50 each'!

William Stewart

The head teacher of Blackburn Public School for the first thirteen years was William Stewart, a pillar of Blackburn UF Church, and active in village affairs. The gift of the Baillie Institute and Reading Room came through his intervention, and he also obtained from the philanthropist thread-maker, Coats of Paisley, 500 books to be added to the village library, and 120 pairs of spectacles to be distributed among the elderly of Blackburn – a welcome gift in the days before the Welfare State.

The school board schools were non-denominational, and if no separate provision was made for Catholic children, then all the children went to the 'Public.' A Catholic school was set up in 1880 under the supervision of the Bathgate priest, but it lasted only until 1887; not until the 1930s was another Catholic school created in Blackburn, by moving the children of the original board school in Kidd Street to Redhouse School, and converting the Kidd Street school to a Catholic primary, known as Murrayfield School. By 1953, this old school was overcrowded and in poor condition. A new Catholic primary was opened that year in Hopefield Road, by Archbishop (later Cardinal) Gordon Gray – Our Lady of Lourdes Primary School.

Redhouse School, built as Blackburn Public School in 1911.
Violet Carson

Anthony Jordan

Anthony Jordan was the first headmaster of Our Lady of Lourdes RC Primary, taking up his post at the old school in Kidd Street in 1951. A quiet reserved man, he 'lived by prayer and good works done in humility,' though to his pupils he was an imposing figure. His sudden death at the age of 57 after the prize-giving ceremony in July 1966, was a shock to staff and pupils.

With the expansion of Blackburn in the 1950s, Redhouse School reached capacity, and an overflow class was held for a time in the Lindsay Hall. When the huge expansion of Blackburn took place in the 1960s, leading to 41 per cent of Blackburn's population being of school age, the village schools were bursting at the seams. The roll at Redhouse reached 835 in 1963, larger than many a secondary school. Blackburn Primary School opened in 1959, but an extension was needed in 1966, by which time it was spread over three buildings – Redhouse School, Ladeside Road and the infant school in Riddochhill Road. The Catholic primary doubled in size, and Murrayfield Primary School opened in 1964 with capacity for 640 pupils.

Redhouse School class 1952.
Back row (L-R): unknown, Barry Dunlop, William Dunlop, Douglas Cummings, William Black, Ian Watson.
Middle Row: Caroline Reid, Jane Russell, – Stewart, unknown, May MacLaughlan, Margaret Wright, unknown, Edith Dunn.
Front Row: Margaret Drysdale, Nanette Wisby, Sandra MacQue, Irene Hamilton, Russell Hannah, Joseph Fleming, Russell Gibbs, Irene Robertson, Jeanie Wilson, Anne Housley, Mary Wicklow.

Russell Hannah

However, Blackburn's population contracted almost as fast as it had expanded, and by the 1980s, it was obvious that there was an over-provision of primary school places in the village. Our Lady of Lourdes had dropped from its 1960s roll of over 500, to just 123 pupils, and by the 1990s, closure threatened. Its continuing existence was secured by moving the council's library headquarters from Bathgate into the west end of the school buildings in 1997. Since then the roll has grown to 150 (at least partly, it is said, because of non-Catholic parents enrolling their children there in the hope that they will then get into St Kentigern's Academy in Blackburn), and the school is again flourishing, and seeking to recover its lost classrooms. Murrayfield Primary gave up some of its surplus classrooms to the Community Education west area office and a council IT training suite, and its current roll is 162, plus nearly 60 in its nursery class. Blackburn Primary was concentrated on the Riddochhill Road site. After 74 years as a school, Redhouse closed in 1985, and its handsome building was converted into flats.

Blackburn Academy

Secondary school provision, both non-denominational and Roman Catholic, was provided for the expansion of the 1960s. Until then, Blackburn's secondary pupils went to Bathgate. Blackburn Academy opened in January 1972, with just a first and second year. Each year brought a new intake and after five years, the school had its full six years. With the catchment area taking in Blackburn, Seafield, Stoneyburn and the Deans area of Livingston, it was not long before huts had to be built in the grounds to accommodate all the pupils.

Blackburn Academy was a pleasant, light, airy building, designed round a quadrangle, with 'off-shoot' wings for noisy activities such as technical education and PE. The Assembly Hall, with its fine acoustic, was regularly used by West Lothian Schools' Orchestra and brass bands for rehearsals and concerts. A 25-metre swimming pool was provided, as was a vehicle entrance to the technical rooms, so that pupils could learn car mechanics. It was a well-planned and well-equipped school, and the pupils were generally appreciative of it and did not abuse it. There was a small proportion of difficult cases, but the general attitude among the children was good, homework was done, and their attitude to teachers was co-operative.

The school could accommodate 1,150, but when James Young High School opened in 1983 and the Livingston pupils transferred, the numbers dropped by half. Some of the more academic children were lost, but with smaller class sizes, discipline was simpler, and it was easy for the staff to get to know each child and something of their family circumstances.

Annual summer trips to France and Germany gave the Blackburn children a window on the wider world. Extra-mural activities were available in plenty – sports, music, clubs – and each first year class experienced a residential outdoor education course. In an area of deprivation, the children took enthusiastically to every charity project, filled boxes for pensioners at Christmas, and gave generously to fund-raising activities.

The school's 'special class' was a notable success at keeping less gifted children within mainstream schooling. Those with a special aptitude for one particular subject had the opportunity to join the mainstream class for that subject. Some of these children were given the chance to help with the youngsters at Pinewood School, and the seriousness with which they took their responsibilities was heartening for the teachers. The success in this field encouraged the setting up at Blackburn Academy of the Special Unit for pupils with social, emotional and behavioural problems who had been excluded from other schools or referred by the Psychological Service. With its good teacher/pupil ratio and small tutor groups, Blackburn achieved some success in rehabilitating these difficult cases.

Dr Valentine

The first rector was Dr James Valentine, who came to Blackburn after spells at Bathgate and Armadale Academies. He was a rather distant figure, with whom pupils generally only came into contact if they got into trouble. No regular assemblies were held; instead announcements were made over the tannoy system by his depute, Tom Simister. When it rained, the children were allowed to stay inside the school at breaks – since, as Mr Simister invariably announced over the tannoy, 'the weather is inclement.' Such was Dr Valentine's commitment to the comprehensive system, and his antipathy to singling out pupils for any reason, that there were no prefects and no prize-givings.

In 1985, Dr Valentine retired and was succeeded by Peter Simmons, a more visible, 'hands-on' rector, who favoured a consultative style of leadership. Almost as soon as he took over, the Academy came under threat of closure. The small roll made it more difficult to offer a wide range of subjects. Attempts to bus the children to other schools for subjects not viable at the Academy were not popular with either pupils or parents.

The decline in population throughout the 1970s and 1980s caused as many problems for the school authorities as the earlier expansion. In the mid 1980s, Lothian Regional Council considered closure of the Academy, but a vigorous campaign under school council chairman, John Murray, successfully fought off this first threat. A Teaching Development Centre was located in the school to take up part of the surplus accommodation, but by 1991, the fifth and sixth year pupils together made up only 22. Lothian Regional Council Education Committee mounted a consultation process with the local people, but school board chairman Phyllis Walker complained that the council's mind was made up from the start. No amount of local campaigning to keep the school open – and there was widespread support – could alter the fact that the school was only one third full.

The social reasons for retaining the school were surely strong arguments. The school was a focus of activity and learning in an area of multiple deprivation; it encouraged good school/parent liaison; its facilities were well-used by the public and community groups in the evenings – in 1991, 37 adults were attending classes, and there was a staffed crèche, a women's liaison worker, an adult lounge and an adult users' committee. It was the newest of the four schools in the west of the county, and was in good condition. A caring staff who knew each child personally and small teaching classes were great benefits to an area of social deprivation. Closure meant the loss of a large body of professionals in a place with generally low educational expectations, and loss to the community of one of its main marks of worth and viability. One observer called the closure 'an appalling thing to do to the community.'

But there was to be no reprieve: in July 1992, Blackburn Academy closed. The Blackburn pupils transferred to Bathgate Academy, and the Stoneyburn children to Whitburn Academy. The swimming pool remained open to the public until it required major repairs; then it too was closed. The vandals moved in, and after several break-ins and fires, the building was demolished. Private houses are now being built on the site.

St Kentigern's Academy

St Kentigern's Academy, 2005.
Brian Cavanagh

With its much larger catchment area, St Kentigern's RC Academy was not so badly affected as Blackburn Academy by the decline in Blackburn's population. St Kentigern's opened in 1973 and its catchment area comprises Blackburn, Bathgate, Linlithgow, and the south west of the county. In 1991 the roll was 742; today it is 1,100, and with the huge programme of new house building in West Lothian, it is expected to rise to 1,400. To accommodate the increase an extension – the Almond Suite – was opened in 1998, and in 2002 a fitness suite and 20-metre swimming pool were added. St Kentigern's is one of five schools that will be refurbished during the second phase of West Lothian council's Public Private Partnership programme. The work will provide new classrooms, bus parks, a library, a music recording studio, an administration block, pupil social areas, and a floodlit all-weather pitch. The project should be complete by October 2006.

John Vallely

The first rector of St Kentigern's was John Vallely, who held the post from the school's opening in May 1973 until his retiral in 1983. He was well-known in the teaching profession, was chairman of the General Teaching Council for Scotland, and president of the Scottish Secondary Teacher's Association, as well as serving on numerous other professional bodies and committees. He died just a year after retiring.

The school board and a principal teacher's post with special responsibility for community links help to involve the parents and community in the school and keep open the channels of communication. A wide range of out-of-school activities is on offer to the pupils, and the school's facilities are available for hire by local community groups, such as Roberta Clark's swimming club, which has taught hundreds of Blackburn children to swim over the years. The school puts great emphasis on Christian values, and for this reason has attracted non-Catholic pupils whose parents wish their children to be educated in this ethos. Certainly the school has an enviable reputation for the good behaviour of its pupils and constantly strives to raise academic attainment.

An inspection of St Kentigern's Academy by HM Inspectors of Schools in 1998 produced a very favourable report, especially commending the leadership and management of the school under head teacher Mrs Catherine Gibbons, the accommodation and facilities, and the school's caring and orderly ethos.

Pinewood School

West Lothian prided itself on being among the more advanced counties in its treatment of mentally handicapped people. In 1967, the county council opened Scotland's first purpose-built adult occupation centre. The new building, next to the Almondvale old people's home in East Main Street, could accommodate 90 trainees, who were taught to make a range of products – rugs, furniture, lampshades, knitted goods, toys, pottery and wrought iron work. This adult day centre is about to be replaced by a purpose-built facility in the centre of Livingston.

East end of Blackburn showing Blackburn Academy top left, Pinewood School centre, above the parish church, and Redhouse School (far right) c.1990.

Airpics

Mentally handicapped children attended the Junior Occupation Centre at Gogarburn until the opening in 1967 of the county's first specialist school, Pinewood. It too was built in Blackburn, because of the town's central location in the county and its many facilities – the senior occupational centre, library, community centre, and the adjacent Blackburn Academy. A close relationship developed with the Academy, and Pinewood children used the facilities and swimming pool at the school. The school could accommodate 60 children between the ages of five and eighteen, and from the start, efforts were made to integrate the school with the local community. The school continues to flourish, and takes children through their whole educational career.

CHAPTER 18

Churches

BLACKBURN WAS PART OF Livingston parish, so from an early date local people attended Sunday worship in the old church at Livingston Village, and came under the supervision of the parish minister and Kirk Session. Education and poor relief were supervised by the Session, as were the morals of the people. Kirk Session minutes for Livingston survive from the 17th century and record a wide variety of wrongdoing: blasphemy, drunkenness, Sabbath breaking, discord, even witchcraft and charming. The cases provide rare glimpses of the lives of ordinary people.

In April 1807, 'A Complaint having been made to the Kirk Session against John Edmonstone, Residenter in Blackburn, for harbouring vagrants and disorderly persons in his house and together with them profaning the Lord's Day with drinking and Dissipation, to the great disturbance of his decent and regular neighbours, the Kirk Session order him to appear... John Edmonstone... confessed the charges against him and expressed sincere sorrow for his conduct and promised that he should be upon his guard to give no offence by similar conduct in future.'

An 1825 case concerned Jane Bell of Blackburn, who persisted in accusing John Turnbull, a Blackburn draper, grocer and widower, of being the father of her child, though he as firmly denied it. She applied to the Session to look into her case, as she was not able to support herself and her child. Witnesses were called and asked if they ever saw Jane Bell go to John Turnbull's shop at 'improper hours.' Jane claimed she had been sent to him one evening by her employer, to buy 'a bottle of small beer and a penny candle,' but no witness had anything incriminating to report. Finally it emerged that Jane Bell had already told another man, William Keir, that she was 'with bairn to him, more that she was with child of twins' and 'William Keir got up in a great passion... and declared that he would not have his character blundered through the town upon her account...' The Kirk Session wisely agreed 'to let this matter lie over till God in his providence be pleased to throw more light on this subject.'

In 1824, a Congregational chapel was set up in Blackburn, with John Hamilton as its first pastor. He was succeeded in 1829 by John Boag, under whom the congregation reached 40 or 50. John Boag (1775–1863) later achieved distinction as a lexicographer. After leaving Blackburn, and when in his seventies, he compiled the *Imperial Lexicon of the English Language*, a massive two-volume dictionary which was published about 1847 and achieved enormous sales.

Because the chapel was wholly dependent on the givings of its congregation, it was at the mercy of the economic prosperity of Blackburn. In May 1836, a number of local people left Blackburn (probably because of lay-offs at the foundering flax and spinning works), and again in 1840 the closure of the flax works caused many families to leave. Mr Taylor, the then minister, 'became discouraged and precipitately resigned.' Thereafter the chapel had only '11 joined members' who could no longer maintain it and the minister's stipend of £35 a year, and the congregation was wound up in 1843. Nevertheless, the little Blackburn congregation produced a minister, Nisbet Galloway, who became a much respected preacher in Dunfermline. Some sort of congregation seems to have continued at Blackburn, and John Aird bought the building and used it as a general mission station independent of any denomination, until about 1860 at least.

By the 1830s, the village of Blackburn was thriving, and was the largest centre of population in the parish of Livingston, but was three and a half miles from the parish church in Livingston Village. In September 1836, the minister, the Rev. J.M. Robertson, requested that the church 'be removed about a mile or two miles west... as the great body of the congregation are in the west.' He pointed out that attendances would be better, and so offerings would be greater. But the heritors were 'unanimously of opinion that the removal of the parish church from its present situation to any other part of the parish is quite unnecessary and unexpedient.' The following year, a petition was sent to the heritors from some Blackburn residents asking for the church to be moved to 'a place nearer Blackburn, for the accommodation of that part of the Parish.' But the heritors were still of the opinion that such a removal (with the consequent expense of building a new church) was unnecessary.

Probably as a result of the petition by the inhabitants, the Church of Scotland set up a chapel of ease in Blackburn about 1838 – for the ease of parishioners in getting to a convenient place of worship. At first, services were held in the village school, but subscriptions were raised and the former chapel of the congregational worshippers was acquired in the 1860s. To maintain the dignity of the Established Church, the minister's stipend was £20 higher than the dissenting minister's had been. In 1877, during the tenure of the Rev. Mr Stewart, a belfry and bell were erected on the south gable; the tolling of the bell announced the time of worship at noon on Sundays. In the difficult times after the burning down of the Cotton Mill, with the decline in population of the village, the annual givings at the chapel fell from £50 to £18, Mr Stewart left Blackburn, and the chapel of ease was reduced to mission status, with no ordained minister.

In 1887, the Rev. John Lindsay came to Bathgate as minister of the United

Presbyterian Church, and because he had a good few members in Blackburn, he began to hold an occasional evening service in the village hall (now the Gospel Hall). By 1891, the population had recovered from the loss of the Cotton Mill and was again on the increase. Mr Lindsay and the minister of Whitburn Free Church agreed to co-operate in the establishment of a mission in Blackburn and Seafield.

The Blackburn mission station, under a succession of ministers, was supervised by the Rev. John Lindsay. The United Presbyterian Church and the Free Church united nationally in 1901, so henceforth, Blackburn was part of the United Free Church. In 1905, the Rev. James Kerr was appointed to Blackburn after missionary service in Old Calabar, West

The Rev. John Lindsay (right) and his wife present medals to Redhouse dux winners, Sarah O'Hagan and Edward Clarke, 1928. The other man is Jock Blake.
John McLaren

Africa, as a colleague of the famous Mary Slessor. He was a successful minister, building up a Band of Hope with over 150 children, and a Bible class with over 70 young people on a weekday evening. With a growing membership, it was decided that a purpose-built church should be erected. Fund-raising began, and each member was asked to subscribe £1 – about half a week's wages in those days. Sales of work and concerts were held, and much assistance was given by the members of St John's Church in Bathgate. Over £1,000 was raised, and the church was built and opened in 1908.

The congregation petitioned to become a full charge of the UF Church and this was granted in 1910. The church was a centre of social life – children's organisations, Bible class, a rambling club, a cricket club, a girls' association, and a singing class, which could muster a choir of 50 voices for concerts of sacred and secular music. A Sunday school was reformed, and the annual picnic became a great event for the village children.

In 1929 the national union of the Free Church and the Church of Scotland took place and Blackburn became a congregation of the Church of Scotland. Though no longer having responsibility for Blackburn, the Rev. John Lindsay continued to take an interest, and in 1936 gifted the old chapel to the church. He had bought the hall shortly after it had ceased to be used by the Church of Scotland mission. It was named the Lindsay Hall in his honour, and served as a church hall. Though the Lindsay Hall was enlarged in 1959, it was still not adequate for the needs of the growing congregation. The church considered building on the Trinleyknowe site, but eventually decided on a new hall adjacent to the church. The Lindsay Hall was sold, thus ending its 150 years as a church building.

Blackburn Parish Church, 1996.
Jean Fooks

Throughout the 1930s, 1940s and 1950s, the church flourished, a centre for the social as well as spiritual life of the village. In 1964, the Rev. Arnold Fletcher was inducted to Blackburn Church. But churches throughout the land were about to enter more difficult times. From the 1960s onwards, attendances declined, young people especially deserted the churches, and financial difficulties accumulated. Blackburn was not immune to these changes. During Mr Fletcher's 33-year ministry in Blackburn, the congregation reached its highest point, then gradually aged and declined. Having been inducted to Blackburn before a compulsory retirement age of 70 was introduced for ministers, Mr Fletcher chose to stay at his post into old age, and his pastoral care made him well thought of in the community. He retired in 1997 at the age of 84 and died three years later.

In 1999, the Rev. Dr Robert Anderson was inducted to Blackburn. A bizarre episode enlivened the early days of his ministry, when drugs were found in a heating duct of the church. The drugs squad raided the church on Blackburn gala day and arrested the then organist.

The Church of Scotland in Blackburn today is in good health. Since 1999, the parish has included Seafield as well as Blackburn, and the present membership is just over 550, with an active kirk session of 34 elders, thirteen of them women. The minister has chaplaincy responsibilities in Murrayfield, Blackburn and Seafield Primary Schools and is on the chaplaincy team of Bathgate Academy. Occasional services are held at Almondvale Gardens and Mosside Court Sheltered Housing complexes, and the church organisations are flourishing. The Men's Association and the guild hold regular meetings, and the minister commends the 'superb leaders' of the young people's organisations attached to the church – the Sunday school, youth club, Boys' and Girls' Brigades and Scouts.

Gala day children in front of the old village hall, 1914. Now the Gospel Hall.
John McLaren

The Gospel Hall

When the Miners' Welfare Hall opened in 1925, the village hall (formerly the village school) was purchased by a group of Christian Brethren, some of whom had been converted at a recent evangelistic tent mission at the West End of Blackburn. Though without a formal pastor to lead it, the group continues to this day, independent and self supporting, and finding leadership and teaching within its own membership. A women's group is in existence, and it is hoped soon to restart the Sunday school. Some 35 are in full fellowship, and the Blackburn Christian Brethren are hopeful of further expansion. They have in their care one of the oldest buildings in the village (though its present appearance dates from its renovation as a public hall in 1876), and it is fitting that such a building is still in regular public use and well cared for.

The Scouts had their own hall, but suffered cruelly from vandalism. While it was still brand new, the hall was destroyed by fireraising. Insurance rates soared to a level well beyond the means of the group. The Scouts were given permanent accommodation in the church hall, in exchange for the old Scout hut which stood on church land. The land is now to be sold for development, and the money raised will pay for a new manse. The congregation is not wealthy, but is solvent, thanks to the generous giving of its members. The minister is optimistic about the future, believing the church still to be of importance to the village. He commends the sense of community in Blackburn and has 'never enjoyed so much laughter and fun.'

The Catholic Church in Blackburn

Irish immigration to Blackburn in the 1860s and 1870s resulted in a substantial Catholic population in the village. To attend Mass they had to go to the chapel in Bathgate, until in 1905 it was announced that a Roman Catholic parish was to be established, covering Blackburn, Livingston, East Whitburn, Whitburn and Stoneyburn. The priest, Father Bernard Eardley, was based in Whitburn, but celebrated Mass in Blackburn. The Picturedrome, the Lindsay Hall and the Village Hall were each used for worship on occasion in the early days.

In 1917, Father Rattray took over responsibility for Whitburn, Armadale and Blackburn. During his time, the Catholic church was built at the west end of the village. The church was at first floor level, approached by a long flight of steps, and beneath was the hall. The church opened in June 1924, with great celebrations. Some 1,000 people took part in a procession through the village, accompanied by a

The Catholic chapel in West Main Street, destroyed by fire in 1954.
West Lothian Council Libraries

band, and members of the Ancient Order of Hibernians. During the services, 120 children were confirmed, and the church was dedicated to Our Lady of Lourdes. After Father Rattray's death in 1925, Blackburn was served by Father Michael Whelahan, during whose time Armadale and Blackburn missions were divided. Father Whelahan went to Armadale, and Father William Quigley came to Blackburn mission (including Whitburn) in May 1928. The Blackburn priests continued to live at Almondbank, Whitburn.

In 1937, Blackburn was erected into a parish covering Seafield, Blackburn, East Whitburn, and Whitburn. A chapel of ease, St Joseph's, was built in Armadale Road for the Catholic population of Whitburn, and Father Patrick Lynch was given the assistance of a curate to cope with his heavy workload. In 1949, Father Lynch moved to Fife, and just a few years later, the parish of Blackburn was divided, with Whitburn being given its own parish priest.

The new Blackburn priest was Father Michael McNulty, who was to be a leading figure in the town during a period of great change. He came to Blackburn during the time of austerity following the war. Rationing was still in effect, there were few shops, and Blackburn was a mining village. The growing congregation wanted its new priest to be resident in Blackburn, so application was made to build a house for him. Because of the post-war restrictions on house building, it was agreed that half of the house should be built in 1950, and the other half when building supplies became more plentiful. 'Visitors to Blackburn,' wrote Father McNulty in his short history of the chapel and village, 'are puzzled by the shape of the house and the explanation is that it was never completed.'

In the early years of his pastorate, chapel affairs were flourishing; the church was renovated, but it was still bursting at the seams. A Catholic youth club was active, as well as a Woman's Guild and an enterprising theatre group led by Mary Owens. On the morning of 9 March 1954, the church caught fire and was almost totally destroyed. Alternative premises for services had to be found: Mass was celebrated at the hairdresser's shop at the Cross on weekdays, and in the Miners' Welfare Hall on Sundays. The hall below the burnt-out church was adapted for use as an oratory, and used for weekday Masses, marriages and funerals.

Fund-raising and weekly congregational collections got underway to pay for a new 400-seat chapel, and work began in 1959 at the new site in Bathgate Road, next to Murrayfield Farm. While it was still under construction, the county council announced that hundreds of houses were to be built in Blackburn for BMC and Glasgow overspill. Before the chapel even opened, it was doubled in size. In 1961, after seven years without a proper church, the new chapel was consecrated by Archbishop Gordon Gray, with 50 supporting clergy and some 900 parishioners in attendance. The materials with which the chapel were built are of the finest quality – oak flooring, walnut pews, a stone and marble altar. The stained glass window of the Apparition of the Virgin Mary at Lourdes was made in Chartres, and the altar (since rebuilt) came from the old Aberdeen Catholic Cathedral. Despite the scope of the building work, the debt was completely cleared by 1968: a tribute, said Father McNulty, to the generous and loyal Catholics of Blackburn.

The Rev. Arnold Fletcher
Blackburn Parish Church

Father McNulty
Blackburn Catholic Church

After 32 years in Blackburn, Father McNulty retired to his native Ireland. A presentation was made to him and his housekeeper, Miss Margaret McBride, who had been with him for over 30 years. 'The fondest memories I have are of the people – whether they have been my parishioners or not. Many say Blackburn's a terrible place but I find the people nice, friendly and helpful,' remarked Father McNulty with the forthrightness which sometimes caused offence. He was a great loss not just to the Catholic community, but to the whole village.

Father John Rogerson came to Blackburn that same year, 1981, and in 1992 was installed as a Canon of the Archdiocese of Edinburgh and St Andrew's. When he left Blackburn in 1995, he was followed by Father Tony MacDonald, and in 2003 by Father Ryszar Holuka, who has under his care the Catholics of both Blackburn and Stoneyburn, and who fulfils chaplaincy duties at the Catholic primary schools in these two villages as well as at St Kentigern's Academy. Membership and commitment to the Catholic Church in Blackburn is still high, and Father Holuka looks forward with hope.

An interesting side shoot of the Catholic Church in Blackburn is the Frederick Ozanam Club, part of the St Vincent de Paul Society. Set up in 1987, its aims are relief of poverty, religious instruction, education and social well-being. Fund-raising social events are held and donations are made to both local and national charities.

Friendly links have been established over many years between the Catholic and Protestant churches in the village. Joint services are held at Christmas and on the World Day of Prayer, and religious and social relations between denominations are harmonious. Until relatively recently, mixed marriages were frowned upon. Greater tolerance, and the loss of the young from both denominations, means that the issue nowadays arises infrequently and is usually resolved amicably.

CHAPTER 19

Crime

UNTIL ABOUT 1700, minor crimes were dealt with by Kirk Sessions, and neighbours' or farming disputes by the court of the baron bailie – in disuse by the 1770s as far as can be ascertained, though a baron bailie still played a minor role as George Moncrieff's agent. By the 18th century, most crime was dealt with by the sheriff court in Linlithgow, and capital crimes by the High Court in Edinburgh.

In Blackburn, serious crimes were rare, but certain murders survive in local folklore. Barbara Fechnie, a servant at Blackburn House, was murdered on her way home from Livingston. Her body was found by a servant a little to the east of the Dean Burn – in a sitting position, 'a wooden stob having been driven right through her body.' The suspected murderer, a worker at Seafield Farm, was never brought to trial, but was said to have been shunned by locals and to have lived out a miserable, solitary life. Barbara Fechnie was reputed to haunt the scene of the crime.

'Fatal Love!, or an account of that cruel and inhuman murder which was committed on the body of Mary Johnston, a young Servant Girl, near Blackburn, on Friday last, July 4th, 1823, by John Watson, Cotton-spinner in the same place, who pretended to be [her] Sweetheart.' Some of the detail is certainly invented, but probably the essential facts, published as a pamphlet within a few days of the murder, and sold for a penny, are true. Mary Johnston was 'born of honest labouring parents who learned her to read [and] write, and bred her up to habits of industry – When old enough she went to service, and lived at several places of reputation. Being a comely woman, she had several sweethearts, and had not attained her 18th year, when she became acquainted with one John Watson.' When Mary became pregnant, Watson refused to marry her. He had taken up with a wealthy farmer's daughter, and Mary had become an embarrassment to him. He decoyed her to a lonely lane and cut her throat. When she was missed, a search was made and her father found her body in a ditch. Watson was suspected and during a search of his house, blood-stained clothing was found. He was arrested and charged with her murder.

The first West Lothian police constables were recruited in 1858, and were on duty at all hours, every day. Their distinctive uniform was a navy blue coat and top hat. A police station was built in Blackburn in 1872, near the foot of the east side of Bathgate Road. By the 1930s, it had become inadequate, but work did not begin on the new police station in East Main Street until 1956 – twenty years after the site had been acquired. The new station comprised two semi-detached houses for the policemen, with a modern office between them – a pleasing architectural arrangement still. Nowadays the police station is only manned during the day. After office hours, calls are put through to the police call centre in Midlothian, which is not considered by local people to be a satisfactory arrangement.

Before the war, Blackburn was a small community: crime was not a concern. 'We never locked oor doors – we'd nothing worth stealing!' Everybody knew everybody; when they got up to mischief, youngsters knew they would probably be found out. Blackburn was fairly free of crime, except for the minor sort – drunkenness, brawling and petty theft. As the town grew after the war, so did the social problems which contribute to crime, and Blackburn today shares in the blight caused by the social isolation and loss of respect in a section of its young people.

The two main concerns in present-day Blackburn are vandalism and drugs. A dedicated police drugs officer for Blackburn, PC Sean Anderson, was appointed in 1999, and the town has experienced several major police drugs raids. The community police constable, Stuart Howie, does valuable work in the town. Vandalism, though less serious, affects a larger part of the population. Much money that could be used more profitably is spent every year on replacing broken windows in public buildings, removing graffiti and fitting barbed wire and shutters. A serious incident happened on Easter Sunday in 2001 when a fire was started at Blackburn Primary School. A classroom was gutted and some £60,000 worth of damage was caused.

In 2004, community wardens were appointed as a pilot project in Blackburn, Boghall, Ladywell and Knightsridge. The focus of the Blackburn wardens, Louise Reid and Neil MacKinnon, is on community safety and prevention of anti-social behaviour. They try to forge links between young people and the wider community, acting as mediators and helping to address the issues raised by young people. The wardens are to be transformed into Environment Enforcement Wardens in 2006.

Councillor Jim Swan believes that the key is to get local people involved, and he points to such projects as the refurbishment of the George V Park, led by Alison Kerr and the Riddochhill Tenants' and Residents' Association, as being an example of what local self-help can achieve. He would like to see more ideas and decisions coming from local people rather than council officers, on the basis that Blackburn people know best what is best for Blackburn. He is also concerned by the problem of reaching disaffected youths – those who reject the many organised activities available to them. Both he and long-serving Blackburn councillor Willie Russell wish to improve road safety in the town, and both are convinced that the community is still strong, thanks to the sterling work of the many local voluntary groups.

CHAPTER 20

Welfare and Self-help

Health

IN 1924, a Nursing Association was set up in Blackburn and East Whitburn to employ a district nurse. Her wages and expenses came from weekly payments by the public, or by deduction from the wage packets of local miners. All who paid had the right to call upon her services when required. A house was built in 1926 for the nurse – the little bungalow in West Main Street beyond the old chapel site – and she was available for sick nursing, home visits, care of pregnant women, childbirth, school clinics, and most of the other tasks of a modern district nurse. The Nursing Association was wound up on the introduction of the National Health Service in 1948.

Until the 1950s, Blackburn had no resident doctor, but was served from practices in Bathgate and Whitburn. The main doctor for the village was Dr Thomas (Tammie) Gilchrist, who lived in Whitburn, but held a surgery in the Baillie Institute, then in the red sandstone house known as Forsyth's building. Dr Gilchrist had been a professional footballer with Motherwell FC, and was a doctor of the old school, not a gentle doctor – in fact one former patient referred to him as a 'butcher.' He could pull teeth when necessary, as there was no dentist in the village. In the 1940s, he was succeeded by his son, Douglas (Dougie), who for a time was joined in the practice by his wife, Margaret. The Gilchrists were succeeded by Dr William Gilmour, who came to live in Blackburn in 1957, and took a keen interest in village concerns. He was 'a gentleman' and 'a lovely man,' much involved in Blackburn life.

After the end of the 1960s, Blackburn gained a new health centre at Ash Grove. The health service provided today by Doctors Macaulay, McKinstry, Merrilees and Black covers Blackburn, Seafield and East Whitburn, and is much valued in a community that has a higher than average rate of long-term illness.

The Baillie Institute and the Welfare

That Blackburn got its Baillie Institute was thanks to William Stewart, headmaster of Redhouse School, who approached Lady Baillie of Polkemmet with the request that she provide an institute such as she had already given to Whitburn, Harthill and Fauldhouse. At a public meeting in 1910, Lady Baillie's factor laid down the

The Baillie Institute in West Main Street. Downstairs were carpet bowling and billiard rooms, a recreation room for draughts and dominoes, a kitchen; and two 'splendid baths' – a boon for the miner in a home with no bathroom. Upstairs were the library, reading room, and caretaker's flat.

West Lothian Council Libraries

terms on which she would agree to make the gift. 'It must be run on temperance lines. It was to be a place where young men and old men could gather and enjoy themselves, and return to their families fitted for their work on the following day.' Women, apparently, were expected to remain at their own hearths.

A site was acquired on the Main Street, opposite the West Calder road end, and a handsome building was erected at Lady Baillie's expense and to the same design as her Fauldhouse Institute. (A fifth Baillie Institute, at Longridge, was completed after her death.) The Blackburn Institute opened in December 1911, under the management of a committee of local men, and with facilities for games, reading, and having a bath – since few local houses at the time had a bathroom.

The money to run the Institute was to come from membership fees, so its success depended on the support of local men. By 1922, industrial depression was having a serious effect on funds, and membership fees were cut to encourage more use. Through the troubled 1920s, the Institute struggled, losing money each year. By 1928, the committee had accumulated a substantial debt and feared the Institute might have to close.

Then in 1931, it was suggested that the Miners' Welfare committee might take over the Baillie Institute, and this happened in 1933. The Miners' Welfare committee had access to national funds, and obtained a grant of £1,500 for improvements to the Institute, including the installation of central heating and electric light. The renovated and enlarged Baillie Institute reopened in February 1936. Part of the take-over agreement was that the Baillie Institute should continue to be run in accordance with Lady Baillie's original wishes – in other words, that it should remain a temperance building.

The decades between the wars were a sociable period, when most people were members of organisations, and attended dances, concerts and public meetings of all sorts. In an era still blighted by poor housing and overcrowding, there was little to keep people at home; they were glad to go out and be entertained in warm and well-appointed public halls. Every meeting, political, religious or social, ended with songs sung by local people, and frequently with a dance.

The Baillie Institute lacked a hall large enough for concerts, dances or public meetings, and the Village Hall (the old school) was growing dilapidated. The Blackburn District Miners' Welfare Committee decided to apply to the Coal Companies' Miners' Welfare Scheme for a grant of £3,000 to renew and enlarge their hall behind the Baillie Institute. The grant would pay for the building; its upkeep would be secured by a penny a week deduction from the pay packets of the local miners. Unlike the Baillie Institute, the Miners' Welfare Hall was for the benefit of women and children as well as men. The enlarged hall was reopened in 1936 by West Lothian's MP, George Mathers.

By 1957, there had been a further rise in the population of Blackburn, with greater expansion planned, and another extension was made to the hall, under the management of committee members John McLachlan and Jocky Rankine. By this time, the tee-total requirement of Lady Baillie's original gift had been set aside, and a bar was provided in the Miners' Social Club room in the Institute. For many years, as Jim Walker's book recalls, the Welfare Hall was 'the hub of Blackburn social life, being available for everything from film shows to dances; from wedding receptions to wakes; from Catholic reunions to orange jamborees; from youth clubs to pensioners' guilds; from rock 'n' roll to bingo.'

When the roof of the Welfare Hall needed repairs, it was decided to undertake a major renovation. The Miners' Welfare Club moved out of the Baillie Institute and into the refurbished hall in 1971. The Baillie Institute was sold to the Orange Order for a social club. The committee of Adam Lockerbie, John McLachlan, Douglas McFarlane and Richard Wallace was the driving force behind the improvements, but times were hard for licensed clubs, especially in Blackburn, where there was plenty of competition. The 305 Social Club in the Baillie Institute closed in 1988, and the Miners' Welfare Club closed in 1991. Both buildings have been demolished.

War Memorial

In 1925, Blackburn War Memorial – a granite plaque bearing the names of the 24 Blackburn men killed in the First World War – was fixed to the front wall of the Baillie Institute. A more ambitious memorial had been hoped for, but the wage cuts of the 1920s meant that only £60 was collected from local people. It is possible that a second plaque was added to the front of the Baillie Institute after the Second World War, but no mention has been found of it. In the 1990s, after ten years of fund-raising and voluntary effort by a number of local people, a proper war memorial was erected. Depute head teacher at Murrayfield Primary School, Bill Millan, a qualified art teacher, designed a striking modern war memorial for Blackburn, which was erected in front of Almondvale Old People's Home, and has been retained in front of Almondvale Gardens. The inspiration for the design was battlefield burial – a rifle with fixed bayonet thrust into the ground above a makeshift grave. The granite plaque from the Baillie Institute and another plaque for the dead of the Second World War have been incorporated into the base.

The Elderly

Until 1930, elderly Blackburn people who could no longer support themselves and had no family to provide for them were likely to end up 'on the parish' – a humiliating fate. When the Welfare State was established, it brought a more enlightened way of treating the elderly. The first purpose-built old people's home in West Lothian – Almondvale – opened in Blackburn in 1964. But ideas on care of the elderly have changed again over the last 40 years: it is now considered important to keep them as independent as possible, and so Almondvale Home has been demolished and replaced with Almondvale Gardens – a partnership between West Lothian council and various housing and health agencies. All the flats include smart technology to ensure the safety and independence of the frail, elderly residents. In 1984 a sheltered housing complex run by the Bield Housing Association opened in Mosside Road.

Blackburn Scottish Old Age Pensioners Committee in the 1950s.
Back Row (L-R): Mrs Pearson, Mrs Thompson, Mrs McCulloch, Joe Fleming, Mrs McDonald, Jocky Rankine, Mrs Millar, Mrs Annie Russell, Adam Lockerbie.
Front Row: Mrs Lightbody, Mrs Grantham, Mrs Bell, Mrs Lockerbie, Mrs Agnes Russell.

Blackburn Family Centre

In 1985, the Save the Children Fund, in partnership with Lothian regional council, started up a Young Families Project in Blackburn. Project workers organised a varied weekly programme for parents and under-fives, much of it aimed at improving their general health. The mothers themselves raised funds to subsidise holidays, equipment and activities. Save the Children funding came to an end in 1997 (though it awarded a lump sum of £30,000 on its departure), at which time a local committee took over the running of the centre, with support and funding from the National Lottery and West Lothian council. Led by project managers Tracey Johnston and, later, Sam McCartney, the Centre continued to offer support and activities to local families, with a special interest in encouraging healthy eating, exercise and education.

For a time, the Centre was unfortunately fragmented in three sites – a classroom in Our Lady of Lourdes Primary School, a hut behind the school, and a unit in the shopping centre. Also unfortunate was the need to reapply for funding every three years, which prevented long-term future planning. In 2000, the Trinleyknowe old people's centre was handed over to the Family Centre for a nominal rent, and

Sam McCartney and the management committee have ambitious plans for the future. The Family Centre has tended to be seen as a children's centre, but the management aims to make it a community development centre for adults, with full-time childcare available free to members. The remaining childcare places will be offered to non-members at normal commercial rates, and this income will make the childcare service self-supporting, leaving the grant money to be applied to training and development work among adults. This centre is a considerable asset to Blackburn and strives to fulfil its remit to aid the economic and social development of the town.

BLES

Blackburn Local Employment Scheme was set up in the difficult days of the 1980s, when more than one in four Blackburn people were unemployed. The scheme began in 1982 with a staff of three and eight trainees, and its first and long-serving chairman, Owen Murdoch, was determined from the start that the scheme should be for the benefit of the trainees, and should never decline into a supply of cheap labour for employers. The trainees were trained in painting and decorating skills, and used these new skills for the benefit of local people – the elderly, disabled or unemployed, and low income families. Based at first in the Community Block on the Murrayfield estate, the scheme moved in 2000 to new premises on the Whitehill Industrial Estate.

BLES now focuses on school leavers, who for a variety of reasons have failed to benefit from a formal school education. Joinery, motorbike maintenance, plumbing, roofing and IT have been added to the training on offer, and guidance is given if the trainees wish to acquire other trades; but equally important is the training in life and social skills which will make these 'challenged' teenagers employable. A pool of businesses take the trainees on six month placements, and the placements turn into proper jobs in a remarkable 70 per cent of cases. Fifty-six young people are currently in training, under a staff of ten led by general manager John Ewart, who came to BLES after a distinguished career as Scottish chief executive of the clothing retailer, Next, and whose energy and commitment are undimmed after twenty years in the job. The scheme is funded by Scottish Enterprise Edinburgh and Lothians, and must prove its worth every year to ensure funding for the next. Since it started, BLES Training has helped over 2,000 youngsters, and John Ewart attributes its success to the outstanding work of every member of the BLES team and to its excellent committee of local people.

Blackburn's Libraries

Scots gained an early reputation for having a thirst for books and learning, and the fact that Blackburn weavers and tradesmen in the mid 18th century were willing to spend some of their hard-earned money on a book of poetry by schoolmaster Alexander Cuthbertson shows that more than basic literacy had been attained by ordinary local people by that time.

A parish subscription library was in existence in Livingston by the mid 1840s – not a building, but a collection of books borrowed by the members in rotation, and funded from the subscription fees. The collection consisted of some 300 volumes, but the fee must have been a deterrent. In 1896 a free library was set up in the old Blackburn village school, consisting of 540 volumes bought with money donated by local people. The stock was later transferred to the Baillie Institute, but because no provision had been made for adding new stock, use gradually dwindled until the books were disposed of in the 1930s. What was needed was a public library: well-stocked, free, and open to all.

The Education Act of 1918 gave county councils powers to provide a library service, and West Lothian's county library service began in 1924. Boxes of books were sent to Redhouse School (and later, the Miners' Welfare), and were exchanged two or three times a year. A branch library was opened in the Institute in 1937, under the care of Mr Peggie, the Blackburn headmaster. This service continued until the building of the new library in 1966.

Blackburn Library is architecturally unusual – circular, with light pouring in from the high windows. Today it provides not just books but also videos, DVDs, CDs, talking books, community information, IT tuition and free internet access. A Blackburn reader, Mrs Anne Gilbride, is the most prolific borrower of books in the whole of West Lothian. In early 2007, the library will move to new premises in the Mill Centre and will operate jointly with the Council's Customer Information Services. West Lothian council library HQ relocated to Blackburn in 1997, to the west wing of Our Lady of Lourdes Primary School, bringing to the village the extensive collections of the West Lothian Local History Library, which attract visitors from all over the country, and many from abroad who are researching their family trees.

Self-help – friendly societies, banks and credit unions

Perhaps the earliest secular organisation in Blackburn was the friendly society which was set up in 1799 and 'has been of much benefit to its members, whose numbers are 30 at present, and their stock amounts to 125 pounds Sterling.' A

Blackburn Shepherds' Friendly Society members with crooks and plaids, c.1900.
West Lothian Council Libraries

friendly society was intended to provide against illness or infirmity, and to ensure that each member had a decent funeral, rather than a pauper's burial. Each member would pay in a small amount every week, and in the event of being unable to work through sickness or old age, he would be given a small allowance from the Society's funds. If he died, his widow was given enough to pay for the funeral. But many of the societies were small, and their resources limited. It took only a few cases of long-term illness for funds to become depleted, and many of the early societies, including, apparently, Blackburn, ended up insolvent.

Another 'Blackburn Friendly Society' was set up in 1842, and its regulations show it to have been well organised. New members had to be recommended by two existing members, and had to be 'men of sober character, not above the age of forty years, nor under the age of sixteen; of a sound healthy constitution, free from any secret bodily disease, capable to gain their livelihood by their own industry.' Entry money was twelve shillings, plus quarterly payments of one shilling, so it was not for the poorest in the village, but rather for the respectable and well-doing who wanted to ensure that they did not end up destitute. If a member was found to have caused his illness by 'drunkenness, quarrelling or fighting, or the venereal disease, or any other intemperance,' he got nothing. In 1842, the founding members of this respectable organisation included four members of the Wallace family, William Mungle, and John Turnbull, the grocer who denied he was the father of Jane Bell's child back in 1825. The society lasted only until 1854, then was wound up, and its funds disbursed to members.

Yet another local friendly society, the Blackburn Friendly and Deposit Society, was in being in the 1880s, with well known local names among its office bearers – Dunlop, Russell, Bryce, Hannah, Young, and Anderson.

The resources of a nationwide movement were a better guarantee of financial security than a local society, and from the mid-19th century, a number of large societies grew up, such as the Gardeners and the Foresters. Apart from financial insurance against misfortune, the friendly societies had an important social role, holding social meetings, processions and concerts; and they developed ceremonies, regalia and mysteries similar to those of the Masonic movement. In Blackburn, a branch of the Loyal Order of Ancient Shepherds was set up in 1893. 'Shepherdry,' reported the *West Lothian Courier* in April the following year, 'has become the rage, and has taken the village quite by storm.' At the end of the first year, there were just over 100 members, contributing one pound each per year, or about 6d per week – not a huge sum, but enough to disqualify the poorest workers in the village.

A lodge of the Independent Order of Good Templars (originating in America) was in existence by 1896, and was active in advocating temperance in Blackburn. The Almond Lodge of Templars was wound up after the introduction of the Welfare State in 1948, which made private social insurance unnecessary.

In 1887, a Blackburn Savings Bank was set up in connection with the National Security Savings Bank of Glasgow. Some 163 accounts were opened, and total weekly deposits were about £8, so the average amount saved each week was about 1s 2d. It was a savings bank for the more prosperous working people, and the *West Lothian Courier* commended it as 'a certain means of securing... a noble independence, and making provision for old age and hard times.' It can be seen as part of the strong 'self help' movement of the Victorian era, with aims similar to those of the friendly society movement.

'Self-help'

Robert Boyd Fowlds, treasurer of the Blackburn Friendly Society Savings Bank in 1895, interpreted self-help a little differently, and helped himself to the sum of £60 before disappearing along with two large boxes marked 'Anchoria.' Constable McCrae got on the trail, and found that 'Robert Boyd' had booked a passage on the Anchoria liner for New York. A cablegram was sent, and when the ship called at Moville in Ireland, a police constable was waiting to arrest him.

In 1897, the sub post office in Blackburn set up a savings bank, which was open from 8am to 8pm every weekday. In 1920, the Commercial Bank of Scotland began to offer a banking service for an hour and a half on Thursday mornings at the Baillie Institute. But for a proper bank, Blackburn had to wait until the 1960s expansion. The National Commercial Bank opened a branch in the new shopping centre in 1967. This bank (which later became the Royal Bank of Scotland) remained in operation until March 1997. Its closure left Blackburn without any banking facilities, which, for a town of some 5,000 people, is a major deficiency.

However, in 1994, self-help once more filled the gap when a credit union, a co-operative venture whereby the members can save and borrow even small sums at reasonable rates of interest, was set up in Blackburn and Seafield. Starting out with some 70 members and open for only two hours on a Saturday, the membership has expanded many times over. It now has dedicated offices in the new shopping centre and is open six days a week. In 1997, the interest rate on loans was 12.68 per cent APR, when the more usual commercial rate was three times that figure. The first dividend was paid in 1998, and in 2002 the 1,000th account was opened. So successful has it been that it has taken over the Bathgate Credit Union, and has extended its membership to the whole south west of the county and even as far as Harthill and Eastfield. New collecting points have opened at Addiewell and, most recently, Fauldhouse.

CHAPTER 21

Recreation

UNTIL ABOUT 1900, no formal provision was made by local authorities for children's play in Blackburn. Certain areas were traditional playgrounds: the Happy Valley, along the River Almond to the south of the village; and Eagle Rock, on the south side of the Almond behind East Main Street, reached by a path beside the Dook Raw and a footbridge over the river – a favourite haunt for children in the days when parents were happy to let them play far from home. Other favourite places were the Almond near Southhill Farm, where the river was damned to form a pool some six feet deep; and Paddy's Well in the field beyond the Eagle Rock, where 'water so pure and absolutely freezing just bubbled out of the ground.' Best of all was the Haugh – the flat ground beyond the Almond, on the West Calder road. In 1921, Livingston parish council accepted from Mr Wood of Wallhouse, the former coalmaster, the gift of the Haugh as a recreation ground for the children of Blackburn.

John Meek's trip to the Happy Valley, c.1932.
Violet Carson

The Dooky was a stretch of the Almond behind the present St Kentigern's – once part of the water supply to the Cotton Mill – where many a Blackburn child learned to swim. Another children's haunt of the 1940s and 1950s was the pond near the Latch Pit where large goldfish swam. By stretching under the bars which covered it, the children could catch minnows in a jam jar – though to get there, they had to brave the geese which guarded the nearby farm (now Diesel Jock's). Close by was Seggie's Hill, which was popular for sledging in the winter, though if your sledge didn't stop, you ended up in the Almond.

John Meek

Many people still remember John Meek's annual trips to the Happy Valley. John Meek was a paralysed man with little speech, who lived his life in a basket chair. His neighbours clubbed together to take him on a day trip to the Happy Valley and baked dumplings and other good things to take with them. Gradually the numbers grew until almost the whole village went along. Sports were held and the three Constance sisters entertained on the mandolin. A great fire was lit and the outing lasted into the darkness. In later years, a trip to Portobello was held instead, and it was not unknown for as many as ten buses to leave the village. It was a great day, fondly remembered. In his old age, John Meek was nursed by his sister Jeanie, and he ended his days in Tippethill Hospital.

The Rat(s) Road was the haunt of the men of the village, where 'tossin' took place, accompanied by illegal gambling. The men would hunker down in circles for the game, and if children came near they were 'hunted.'

The King George v Park was planned in the late 1930s and built with the help of a grant from the fund set up to commemorate the king after his death in 1936. The park cost some £1,500 and opened in 1940. There was a large grassy area ideal for rounders and other games, the swings from the Haugh, and a brick shed which is fondly remembered by many Blackburn residents. Each night at ten the gates were locked by the gate-keepers, one of whom, Hugh Miller, lived nearby. The children would leave the park with him then, during the summer, when the nights were long, they would wait until he was out of sight and climb back over the fence to resume their play. 'That was a bad as we got. There was nae badness then. The worst we did was play Kick Door Run Fast.' The metal memorial gates were removed during the war for salvage. After protests to the Ministry of Works, the decision was reversed, but unfortunately the men from the ministry couldn't find the gates, so they were replaced by wooden ones.

It is striking how rural a childhood the older people of Blackburn enjoyed. Their memories are all of playing outside: by the river, in the traffic-free streets, in the fields. They recall the farm horses waiting to be shod at Willie Gray's smithy;

The original metal plaques on the gateposts of the King George V Park have been restored by West Lothian Council and are on display in Blackburn Library.

West Lothian Council Libraries

later Lumsden's garage. They look back with nostalgia, but with the certainty that they enjoyed a safer and freer environment than modern youngsters.

From about the 1880s onwards, working hours decreased, and a half-day on Saturdays gave most workers some leisure time. One week's paid holiday became the norm, and working men at last had the time and the money to enjoy hobbies and organised sports either as participants or spectators. Clubs were formed to cater for every interest, and people enjoyed getting together and making their own entertainment. Musical talent was more valued than it is nowadays, and people were expected to make use of their musical ability by entertaining others.

There were clubs for dancing, rambling, homing, angling, cricket and cycling. A blaes tennis court was laid out by the Forsyths in front of Blackburn House in 1923, but it was a private court, only open by invitation. Carpet bowling was perhaps the most popular sport in Blackburn in the early years of the twentieth century – cheap to equip, suitable for all ages and playable all year round. When the local club won the Browning Cup in 1906, people gathered in the street to see the presentation of the cup, and the club president and vice president were raised shoulder high by the crowd as it 'paraded the street singing *They are Jolly Good Fellows*.' Such an incident shows the importance of sport at that time, and the fondness for communal celebrations, perhaps prompted by the absence of home entertainments.

One of the longest lived sports in Blackburn was quoits. Money prizes attracted competitors from far afield. Betting was commonly associated with the game, and the strenuous exertion of throwing a 10lb–16lb quoit a distance of 18 yards restricted its appeal to men. But in a society of miners who valued physical strength, the champions of the game were highly respected. The quoiting ground was behind the Turf Inn, but the sport declined in the 1930s, and failed to revive after the Second World War.

Since the opening of the community centre in 1966, a fine sports hall has been available to local clubs and individuals, offering a varied programme of activities, with a particular focus on children. Sooner or later, everyone in Blackburn has occasion to visit the Centre – among the attractions on offer are youth clubs, indoor bowling, pensioners' groups, mother and toddler groups, a fitness suite and gym, a computer suite, karate, basketball, roller skating, pool, snooker, table tennis, sequence dancing, aero modelling, and much more.

Cinemas

The Picturedrome was built in 1913, and was the first cinema in Blackburn. It could seat some 600 people – nearly half the Blackburn population. The 'Drome was later taken over by Russell, the haulage contractor, before it moved to its larger premises in Bathgate Road, but its curved roof survives at the entrance to the lane into the council's civic amenity site. A Picture House was run in the Miners' Welfare for many years after the war.

Bowling

Outdoor bowling was late in coming to Blackburn: a bowling club was not founded until 1962, on a green opened by the county council the previous year. A small initial membership of 30 grew and flourished, adding to and improving the facilities as funds allowed. A new clubhouse was opened by Dr Bill Gilmour during the club presidency of Matt Purdie; then a new changing room, and in 2001 a fine new lounge. Meanwhile the bowlers were bringing honour to the club: in 1974, Robert Faulds, Alex Greig and Peter Ball won the British Isles Triples Championships. Peter Ball and Agnes McKay have both been capped for Scotland. Harry Reston had a distinguished bowling career which included 51 caps, a world team gold medal and the Scottish Singles title. His obituary in the *West Lothian Courier* recorded that 'While other bowlers trotted down the green after their bowls, Harry positively chased his, arms flailing on his long, gangling frame, to his stentorian shouts of "Come on, Harry", as if the bowl was an extension of him, as indeed it was.'

Blackburn Bowling Club, Open Grouse Pairs, 1989.
L–R: Ted White, Grouse rep., Andrew Speedie, Alex Murray, Bert Storrie, Robert Cumming, John McCafferty.
John McCafferty

In 2005, the club had the honour of hosting the WLBA Senior Singles and Champion of Champions events. Today the membership is 160 full (bowling) members, and another 90 associate members with the right to use the club's social facilities. Within the last three years, the proportion of younger members has grown and there are 10 youngsters in the junior section. The social facilities are made available to the wider community, and this flourishing club is an asset and a credit to the town.

Football

The first football team in Blackburn was Blackburn Thistle, which was set up in May 1886, and was a founder member of the Linlithgowshire Junior Football Association in 1887–1888. This first club had a short life, as had the Blackburn Rovers team founded in 1891, and two others. The first club to survive for any length of time was a second Blackburn Rovers team, which reached the final of the East of Scotland Juvenile Cup in 1916, and won the Linlithgowshire Cup in 1921. In that same year, it moved from Juvenile up to Junior level. In 1925, the club reverted to the name Blackburn Football Club as it was to become again a 'purely local club.'

In 1932, Blackburn Athletic FC came into being as a junior team, and enrolled that year in the Midlothian League competition. The club secretary was that tireless community worker, Jocky Rankine, and thanks to a grant from the local Miners' Welfare Society, the team was able to build a new pavilion at its Murrayfield Park ground. Despite winning the Midlothian League Championship in 1934, the club was in financial trouble by 1935. A new committee with football stalwart Frank Ogilvie as secretary tried to save the club, but it was wound up in 1937.

Murrayfield Rovers Football Club, 1945.
West Lothian Council Libraries

Perhaps the finest football team to come out of Blackburn was the Juvenile side, Murrayfield Rovers. Undefeated in 1945 and 1946, they won all the silverware they competed for, including the Lord Weir Cup (the Juvenile equivalent of the Scottish Cup). Among that fine team was Freddy Glidden, who later signed for Hearts FC.

In 1958, Blackburn Amateurs FC was formed, and won the Brunton Cup in its first season. In 1964, the New Blackburn Athletic FC was formed, stepping up from 1st Class Juvenile to Junior at the start of the 1964–65 season. The 'New' prefix was to acknowledge the existence of the previous Blackburn Athletic team. The club was one of the few using a public football ground as their home – Murrayfield Park. With the co-operation of the county council and other park users, an agreement was made to give Athletic priority. An experienced committee was formed, benefiting from the experience of many of the incomers to Blackburn in the 1950s and 1960s, particularly secretary Bob Newbury, who was well known in youth football circles. However, by the early 1970s, the team was in decline, and it folded in 1974.

Blackburn community centre supported a youth team, whose under-19 five-a-side team won the Scottish Association of Boys' Clubs' National Championship in 1970. Nine years later, another Blackburn Centre team won both the Scottish and the British Association of Youth Clubs' five-a-side titles: James Brown, Alan Irvine, Billy McFarlane, Steven Mallon, David Swan, and Kevin Bann (substitute).

In 1978, two youth teams, Blackburn Thistle and Blackburn United, agreed to merge. Murrayfield Park was upgraded with help from West Lothian district council, in an effort to step up to junior football. In 1980 Blackburn United was admitted to B division of the east region of the Scottish Junior Football Association. The club struggled financially at first, but was helped by a merger in 1984 with Blackburn Juveniles – a fine team who had previously won the Lady Darling Cup (a Scotland-wide competition).

Blackburn United won promotion and has managed two cup final appearances – in 1988 in the St Michael's Cup, and in 1999–2000 against Fauldhouse in the West Lothian Millennium Cup. A grant from the council helped pay for a covered enclosure at Murrayfield Park for fans, though jokers suggest that the usual gate at Blackburn matches is 'twa men an' a dug.' The football club works in close association with the bowling club, and acknowledges the generous help given by the latter, as well as by many loyal sponsors and supporters, to keep junior football alive in the village. The committee works hard throughout the year to raise the £20,000 or more required annually to keep the team in existence.

In 2001, a new manager was appointed, Michael Lynch, who just failed to take the club into the First Division in 2003. He then joined Celtic's youth development programme and was replaced by Peter Duncan. Today the club has a new mood of confidence under manager John Jamieson. The best known ex-player was Alan Irvine, who moved to Hibernian FC and several well known Scottish and English clubs. More recently, Chris Innes played for Stenhousemuir, Kilmarnock and Dundee United.

Blackburn has seldom achieved outstanding success at football, but has nevertheless had its influence on the game. In 1999, Blackburn United submitted to the east region FA wide-ranging proposals for changing the structure of the junior game. These moves were intended to raise standards and attract more spectators, especially at the top end of the game. The proposals were not adopted but they stirred up the debate and led to the Superleague set-up of today. Blackburn's award-winning match programmes deserve a mention, and taken together they make up a serial history of the club.

One of the great characters of Blackburn football was Alexander (Dixie) MacLachlan. After a distinguished record in the Great War, he became a miner, and was also company Sergeant Major with the West Lothian Home Guard, lollipop man, Redhouse School janitor and attendance officer, Burns enthusiast, and freemason. He devoted 60 years to football as both player and trainer. During these years, he reckoned that he sent 82 players to First and Second Division clubs. Dixie died in 1978, 'one of the last of the worthies.'

Gala Days

Blackburn Gala Day, 1913.
Janette Fowlds and Margaret Wilson

Traditionally, Blackburn is known to have held fairs from at least as early as 1750, though no written records of these exist. The event was a mixture of feeing fair (where farm servants went to offer themselves to new employers, and farmers to find workers), and races: horse races near the Knowe at the west end of the village, and foot races along the Main Street. The event attracted a crowd, so entrepreneurs set up stands selling sweetmeats, fruits, pastries, and trinkets, which 'lined the street of the village on both sides right along.'

An old custom was practised on the night before the fair. 'Gardens were plundered of their cabbage stocks, and all the young people of village betook themselves to the sport of rattling at the doors with 'runts and sticks' and crying 'Doll-oll'. The rattling on doors is said to have served to remind the villagers that fair day was on the following day. Another old custom was the 'cleaning time,' a sort of spring cleaning of the house before the fair. The second Friday in August was the great day, with the feeing fair in the morning and the games in the afternoon and evening.

From about 1835, the horse racing ceased, but foot races and other sports continued in a field. The races attracted the leading 'pedestrians' (runners) and the day was a public holiday for the village. The children assembled at the school, then paraded through the village west to Knowehead, then east to Seafield and back to the school (further than today's youngsters would be prepared to walk!), then were supplied with pies, cookies and sweets. Even after the closure of the mills, the Blackburn games or fair continued, and as late as 1887 there were 21 races for both adults and children, including hurdles, and a mile handicap. There was also a quoiting competition, and Whitburn Brass Band entertained the spectators. The games continued until the First World War made their staging difficult, and they merged with the gala day.

Games were also held annually till about 1912 by the Loyal Order of Ancient Shepherds in Blackburn. After a procession with banners, the games were held in the fields of Blackburn Mains – cycle races, walking and running races, and quoiting; but in 1904 'the football could not be finished owing to some of the players running away with the ball.'

In 1911, the village celebrated the coronation of King George v. The sum of £3 was left over after the festivities and a public meeting decided to spend the surplus on a treat for the children of Blackburn. Thus the first gala day specifically for children was held in July 1912. Five hundred children assembled at the Public School (Redhouse) and marched in procession to a field at Riddochhill Farm. Milk and buns were handed out, then races and a football tournament were held, followed by tea and pastry. Whitburn Band provided musical entertainment.

Blackburn gala day has proved one of the most durable and regular galas in West Lothian, thanks to many hard-working volunteers. It was suspended during the First World War, and the prolonged miners' strike in 1921 caused its cancellation that year and the following year. But it resumed in 1923 and was held every year without a break until 1988, when there were not enough volunteers to undertake the work of organising the day. Happily, it started up again the following year and has been held each year since then. Its long and seldom-interrupted history is perhaps unequalled by any other gala day in West Lothian, and proves the active community spirit that has long existed in Blackburn.

June was the favoured time for the gala day during most of the 20th century:

Children passing Young the baker's dyke, at a gala day in the 1950s. They include Robert Kerr, David Shields, Alan Split (with flag), Tam Meek, and Johnnie Miller (white gutties).

Russell Hannah

a brief move to August in the mid 1950s was unpopular and it reverted to its usual month. During the 1920s, various competitions were introduced for the children, such as fancy dress and best decorated pole. A banner inscribed 'Blackburn Children's Gala Day' was acquired in 1924. In the 1930s a Co-operative gala day was held in addition to the village one. At the 1934 gala, 1,000 children are said to have gathered at Murrayfield and paraded through the streets, many of whose shops and houses were decorated. The sports followed at the Murrayfield park. In 1944, despite the war, three bands attended, and the children were each given cakes, milk and threepence.

In 1953, to mark the coronation of Queen Elizabeth II, it was decided to choose a gala day queen and retinue. The first queen was Christina Anderson, with Marion Thomson as her chief lady in waiting, and the crowning was carried out by Redhouse school teacher, Mrs Young. As the village grew in the 1950s and 1960s, so did the number of children taking part. In the 1950s, some 2,000 children were catered for. Blackburn 'exiles' regularly returned to the village for the gala day and swelled the crowd.

In 1964, the procession of children and uniformed organisations stretched the entire length of Main Street, accompanied by five bands and decorated floats. Queen Avril Drysdale was crowned by Mrs David Bruce, and the sports were held at Murrayfield Park. At the beginning of the 1970s, it looked as though the gala might fail through lack of helpers. The death in 1973 of gala stalwart Jocky Rankine at the age of 90 was another blow. However, a new committee steered by secretary Mrs Grace McCrae breathed new life into it, and the 1974 gala committee distributed 2,500 children's lunch boxes. The queen, Susan Hyndman was crowned by Mrs M. Russell, and an annual trophy for the best decorated premises was instituted in memory of Jocky.

A civic week of events was begun in 1976, and ran successfully for several years. However, by the early 1980s, the civic week events were not receiving the same support, nor was there the same willingness in the community to undertake the necessary hard work in the months leading up to the big day. In 1988, for the first time for over 60 years, there was no gala day in Blackburn. It began again the following year and continues still, in reasonably good health after nearly 100 years. Now that the teachers no longer marshal the children to take part, and the uniformed organisations are less strong, the numbers attending are smaller than in the old days. Newcomers to the town may not have grown up with a tradition of gala days and perhaps do not realise the work and expense involved in organising such an annual event. The money for gala days comes from gala committee fund-raising throughout the year, the generosity of local people, a donation from West Lothian council, and some sponsorship from local businesses. The Murrayfield park is now the site of the bowling club, and today the gala takes place on the sports field. In 2004, Jenna Clucas was queen, with Dean McIndoe as her champion. Her sister Robyn in 2005, and Ashley Graham in 2006, continued the long tradition.

At the time of the demolition of the Miners' Welfare Hall, Jim Wallace rescued the gala day banner. Though damaged, it was restored with a new illustration of an accordion band, painted by a Blackburn Academy pupil. When Jim Wallace went back to retrieve the Shepherds' friendly society banner, he was too late: it had been dumped.

CHAPTER 22

Organisations and Individuals

Organisations

CHURCH-AFFILIATED ORGANISATIONS such as guilds and Sunday schools were some of the earliest societies in Blackburn, and continue to flourish. The longest established women's group in Blackburn today is the Blackburn Women's Social Services Club. It was started in 1944, with the aim of arranging demonstrations of war-time cookery and make-do-and-mend. Sixty years on, it continues to offer a programme of meetings, speakers and demonstrations, based in the Community Centre. Blackburn SWRI began in 1932, with a programme based on cookery, sewing, crafts and other 'home-making' skills, but after many successful years it was wound up.

In 1974, the Trinleyknowe Centre opened as an old folk's centre, offering facilities for those who found the main community centre too big and crowded. Provided for the senior citizens were lounges, a television, dominoes, darts, and even a shower. Most Blackburn pensioners' clubs, however, are run on a self-help basis, by pensioners, for pensioners. Their hard-working secretaries manage to put together a varied programme of meetings year after year. Pennies, a senior citizens' group, meets in Blackburn Parish Church; the Golden Age group meets in the community centre; and the oldest of these groups, the Blackburn branch of the Scottish Old Age Pensioners' Association, dates back to at least 1946.

Young people in Blackburn, as everywhere else, are reluctant to join organised clubs. It is older people who are the office bearers and committee members of the many societies; so what the future holds for the clubs once this generation retires, is uncertain. But it is heartening to consider the great number of groups that meet every week, the unsung charitable work they do, the funds they raise, and the friendship, fun and learning they provide for their many members.

Uniformed Organisations

The first Girls' Brigade was wound up in 1982, but after a gap of nearly 20 years, a new brigade was formed in 2001. It now has some 35 girls and is thriving. The Boys' Brigade succumbed to the particular reluctance of boys to join uniformed organisations. However, the Scouts survive. A troop was formed in Blackburn in the early days of Scouting. In 1954, a new hall was opened for the 15th West Lothian (Blackburn) Scout group. The group has been fortunate in its many hard-working leaders. One of those, Jim Robertston, was awarded the Silver Acorn badge in 1991 for 30 years of service to the Scout movement.

Freemasonry

There have no doubt been freemasons in Blackburn for several centuries, but until fairly recently, they had to look elsewhere to practise their craft. In fact, the ladies were better organised, setting up an Almond Chapter of the Eastern Star in 1922, with Christina Suttie as Worthy Matron. An attempt was made in 1942 to set up a masonic lodge in Blackburn. A committee was formed and money was raised, but nothing came of the scheme, and the funds were donated to the Edinburgh Royal Infirmary.

However, when Blackburn expanded in the 1960s, the newcomers included several masons. They got together in November 1962 as the Blackburn Masonic Club, with the intention of forming a lodge. In 1963 a charter in the name of Lodge Lord Bruce 1601 was granted and meetings began in various halls in Blackburn. None proved satisfactory, so the lodge was formally consecrated in the Seafield Institute on 16 November 1963.

After 11 years in Seafield, the need was felt for dedicated premises for the lodge. Enquiries were made and eventually the Lindsay Hall in Blackburn was purchased from the parish church and converted. It opened on 21 August 1976. Over the last 180 years, this little building has seen service as a chapel, a church, a church hall and now a masonic lodge. Its present appearance gives little indication of its long history, but it's to be hoped that the building will serve for at least another 180 years.

Individuals

James Weir was born in Blackburn, probably in 1843, and was a grandson of Elizabeth Bishop, daughter of Robert Burns, and her husband, John. Weir received his early education at the old village school in the Bathgate Road, but after his father's death about 1850, the family moved to Glasgow. At the age of 15 or so, James Weir became an engineering apprentice, prospered, and set up business in Glasgow with his brother, George, specialising in boilers and engines. The Weir Group became one of the largest engineering firms in Scotland, and currently employs 8,000 people worldwide.

Blackburn worthies at the church door, 1950s.
Back Row (L-R): Jan Smith, Jock Blake, Mr Bailey, Mrs Irvine.
Front Row: Mrs Stark, Jeanie Meek, Mrs Bailey, Jocky Rankine, Mrs Rankine, Mrs Mary Wallace.

Jim Wallace

In 1911, Blackburn was the scene of perhaps the earliest powered flight in West Lothian, when **Alex McCall** of Hopefield Cottage built a bicycle-powered monoplane, and flew it to a height of over twenty feet. Depending on pedal power, the technology failed to catch on, and no more was heard of it.

Willie Hannah was born and bred in Blackburn, and served during the Great War with the Argyll and Sutherland Highlanders. His musical career began with the mouth organ, then he took up the melodeon and the accordion, formed a band, and was in much demand at the many social evenings which took place in Blackburn and further afield between the wars. He and his talented fiddle player, Packy Cadden, are said to have smoked a packet of Craven A between them at each dance.

During the Second World War, Hannah became a Lieutenant in the Home Guard, and served as Bombing Officer of the 1st West Lothian Battalion. On one occasion, he picked up a live grenade which had fallen near his men and threw it away, thus probably saving many lives. A week later, he was seriously injured by a bomb and spent two months recovering in Bangour Hospital. In 1944, he was awarded the MBE. In civilian life, he was head postman at Bathgate post office.

After the war, Willie Hannah continued to entertain with his accordion band, playing at dances and on the wireless – the 'King of the Waltz.' He was a notable figure in the history of the accordion, being responsible for some of the technical development of the instrument, and for the publication of an early teaching manual. He was among the first to make recordings on the instrument, and was the first celebrity accordion player. Some of his tunes are still in use, the best known being *Snow in Summer* and the *Agnes Waltz*. He was one of the great figures of Scottish country dance music, and a major influence on Jimmy Shand and the later generation of musicians. One of Jimmy Shand's waltzes is named after his friend – *Memories of Willie Hannah*.

More recently, other Blackburn people have shown artistic talent. In the mid 1950s, **Rose Goldie** was a member of the Scottish National Opera Company, and a professional singer. More recently, accordionists **Yvonne Mathieson** and **David Wilson** achieved success, as did Pipe Major **Robert Martin**, winner of Scottish, British and European Championships with the Boghall and Bathgate Caledonian Pipe Band. **Dennis O'Donnell** is a well-respected poet who has published two volumes of poetry: *Two Clocks Ticking* (1997) and *Smoke and Mirrors* (2003).

Blackburn even produced its own Billy Elliot: (Alexander) Bruce Simpson. As a boy in the 1960s, he was told to take his wee sister Jane to her ballet classes. After a few weeks, he asked if he could join in – and never looked back. He has danced in South Africa – with the State Theatre Ballet – and in Europe and Hong Kong. Since 2000 he has been artistic director of Louisville Ballet, the state ballet of Kentucky, USA.

Tommy Miller

West Lothian Council Libraries

Tommy Miller was born in 1929, and grew up in Blackburn, a pupil of Redhouse School and the Lindsay High School in Bathgate. He became an apprentice joiner at Whitrigg Colliery, and joined Armadale Boxing Club. His talent was soon evident and he moved to several well-known Glasgow boxing clubs. In his first competitive year, 1945, he won 11 bouts at flyweight. In 1948 he won the Scottish Bantamweight Championship and the British Bantamweight National Coal Board Championships. He was also a reserve with the British Olympic Team. In that one year, 1948, he fought 85 times, winning 73, and losing only eight. In those days, championships were decided in one night, so the boxers might have to fight three bouts in one evening. Miller's many Blackburn supporters also required stamina: often their bus did not bring them home until the early hours of the morning. In 1949, Miller won the British Bantamweight title, the British Boxing Championships, and various other titles, and the magazine *Boxing News* voted him Boxer of the Year. The people of Blackburn presented him with an oak display cabinet in recognition of his achievements. In 1950 he turned professional and continued his success, winning the Scottish Featherweight title, and losing the British Professional title only on a technicality. He retired in 1953, but made a comeback in 1958. When he lost in the 1959 final of the Scottish Bantamweight championships, he decided finally to retire. His brother, **Jackie Miller**, was also a fine boxer, though less well-known, as was **Joe Allan**, a Scottish Welterweight champion.

There are several names that crop up regularly in Blackburn public life that, though now almost forgotten, were the movers and shakers of their day, to whom Blackburn owes a debt for keeping strong its community spirit. **David Prentice** is one of these – he was a Riddochhill miner, the prime mover behind the Miners' Welfare Hall, and active also as session clerk in the church, and in the Loyal Order of Ancient Shepherds. He died in 1955.

Still more active in public life was **John (Jock) Blake**, another Riddochhill miner, who was an organiser of the Blackburn games, a founder member of the gala committee and the Blackburn and District Nursing Association, a leading member of the committee for the building of the parish church, a Justice of the Peace, and a member of the West Calder Co-operative Society board, the Old Folk's Treat committee, the school board, the parish council, and the county council. In his 'leisure' hours, Jock enjoyed quoiting, football and gardening. He died in 1940 aged 74, and was eulogised as Blackburn's Grand Old Man: so few then survived beyond their seventies.

Geordie Baird was an outsize personality until his death in 1951. He was a founder member of the gala committee in 1911, and of the local branch of the ILP, the forerunner of the Labour Party. He represented Blackburn on the board of the West Calder Co-operative Society, and established the annual Old Folk's Treat, which was held for many years on New Year's Day. In his spare time, he was on the committee of the Miners' Welfare Society, and founded the Blackburn branch of the Old Age Pensioners' Association. Geordie liked a drink and brewed his own beer, and many stories are still told of him and his antics. He lived for a time in Douglas Buildings, whose owner, 'Hatchet' Douglas, kept a menagerie of animals and fowls, including a pet monkey. One summer evening at the end of their shift, Geordie and some of his neighbours were sitting out at the back, waiting to have

Geordie Baird, with a young
Mary Ogilvie.
Mary Wilson

a bath to wash off the pit grime. To amuse the others, Geordie said, 'I'm awa tae fight the billy goat.' Down he got on his hands and knees, butting the goat with his head. The goat tolerated it for a few moments, then lowered its head and butted Geordie between the eyes. Down he went, rolling over and over down the steep slope of the back yard – knocked out cold. The next day he had 'two of the loveliest black eyes you ever saw.' Humour in the old days was plentiful, but was often robust. A group of locals was preparing the gala day ground. The wife of a fellow worker brought over a home-made steak pie for her husband; Geordie took it, promising to pass it on; instead he and Jocky Rankine ate it.

Still celebrated in Blackburn folklore is **John Rankine**, always known as Jocky. Jocky was hall-keeper and cinema manager at the Miners' Welfare Hall and named his projector 'Flora MacDonald.' When Flora broke down, he was hard put to it to control the jeering children in the audience. The picture house was run in partnership with the one in Stoneyburn and half-way through the evening, the first film was sent by motorbike up to Stoneyburn, and the second film brought back to Blackburn. If Jocky appeared during the inevitable delay calling for order, he was liable to be pelted with apple cores or worse. He was a great organiser of trips and of treats for the old folk, and a stalwart of the Old Age Pensioners' Association. For many years a leading figure in the gala days, and an indefatigable worker, 'he was in everything except the Woman's Guild,' and was sometimes referred to as the Lord Provost of Blackburn. In 1934, Blackburn Athletic Football Club won the Midlothian League, and for years afterwards he used the League flag as his bed cover. He was a 'great man with the pen' and once wrote to Nellie Melba, claiming he was a poor man who couldn't afford tickets to her Edinburgh concert. Back came free tickets for the Edinburgh Empire and the chance to meet her afterwards! He was one of the best known worthies of the village in his old age – a little man with a walrus moustache and a 'wee flask for medicinal purposes.'

Among the best known of Blackburn's councillors was **Willie Connolly**, whose career culminated as convener of West Lothian district council. He first became involved in local politics at the end of the war, when he was elected to Whitburn and Livingston district council. Two years later, he became a county councillor, representing Blackburn West. He served on various committees and was for many years the finance convener. He became the first convener of the new

West Lothian district council in 1976, but lost his seat the following year. He worked in the mines in his early years, and latterly was the publican of the County Tavern and owner of a taxi business. A forceful character, he was often embroiled in controversy, but did much for West Lothian and for Blackburn.

Jan (John) Opara was a Polish soldier who came to this country during the Second World War, got a job with the BMC in the 1960s, and settled in Blackburn. He became an active supporter of the Scottish National Party and was the first person to suggest that the gala day be extended into a civic week. He was much respected in the village, and was chairman of Blackburn community council, which still promotes Blackburn's interests.

William Gardner, a former pupil of Redhouse Public School, rose to become HM Inspector of Prisons for Scotland and was made a Companion of the Imperial Service Order and awarded the OBE. He died in 2004.

There are many, many others who could and should be mentioned, but perhaps they could form the basis of another book, this time by a native of Blackburn. Among those whose names often crop up in older folk's stories are Busy Peter – Peter Campbell, lamp-lighter, and caretaker at the Orange Club; Nellie McDonald, the district nurse; Nanny Watt and Johnnie Aitken of the Co-op; Tyler Meek – a 'great fisher, but a better drinker'; Tony Constance the barber; Mrs Jessie Hunter, who in 1912 was one of only five lady drivers in West Lothian and who lived to a grand old age; and 'Schoolie' Russell, the Redhouse school janitor.

CHAPTER 23

Blackburn: past, present and future

Blackburn gala day crowd, 1950s.
Alex Russell

BLACKBURN WAS THE FIRST community in West Lothian to be industrialised, with its cotton spinning mill, and then the flax spinning and weaving mills. Why did it not then develop into an industrial centre like Bathgate or Whitburn?

A number of factors combined to curb its prosperity. Water power, which had given Blackburn its early industrial advantage, ceased to be of any importance with the introduction of steam power. By the second half of the 19th century, textiles were a declining industry in Scotland, concentrated mainly in Dundee and in the West. During its textile years, the workforce in Blackburn was mainly female, and mainly youthful – not the sort of workforce that bred entrepreneurs with the status, experience or capital for setting up in business on their own.

The population did not reach the critical mass necessary to attract new businesses by the availability of a pool of workers, and mining soaked up the available male workforce. Nor, with its smaller population, did Blackburn go the way of Whitburn and Armadale and seek burgh status: it continued under the county council, for whom the village was just one of many communities. Blackburn continued to be dependent for shops and services on Bathgate, Whitburn, and later, Livingston. Perhaps there was too much competition in the immediate vicinity for another industrial town to take successful root. The lack of a rail link was probably a further disincentive to the setting up of new industries.

Throughout the 1980s and 1990s Blackburn endured an uphill struggle. By the mid 1990s, Blackburn still showed all the symptoms of a community in difficulties: a high proportion of single parent families, low-paid employment, low car ownership, low house ownership, unemployment at 9 per cent: the third highest level of deprivation in West Lothian.

Despite all the efforts of local people, local councillors, West Lothian council, and many voluntary and statutory bodies, Blackburn is not yet out of the woods. It has a higher than average proportion of pensioners and of lone parent households. Only 60 per cent of Blackburn families have a car, and only 54 per cent of adults have some educational qualifications. Some 25 per cent of adults have a limiting long-term illness, and unemployment stands at 5 per cent, compared with 3.55 per cent in the rest of West Lothian. Almost 25 per cent work in the declining manufacturing sector, but only 14 per cent are in skilled trades. Some 10 per cent work in the construction industry, nearly 15 per cent in wholesale and retail and another 9 per cent in transport, storage and communications; but the number of professional people is well below average.

The population fell from 5,150 in 1994 to 4,761 in 2001, but is expected to rise a little over the next few years, thanks to private house building on the Wester Breich road and the Blackburn Academy site. Vandalism and poor environment are still problems, but much has been done in recent years: trees, shrubs and hedges have softened the bleakness of the Bathgate Road, and pitched roofs will improve the appearance of the Murrayfield point blocks. The growth of private housing in the town should eventually lead to a more balanced social mix of population, and to rising property prices both on the private and the former public sector housing estates.

Village life has changed a great deal over the last 200 years. Once, almost everybody worked in the same industry, whether it was textiles or, later, coal. They lived in company houses, and shared the same experiences and a similar level of income. Today there is no one dominant employer. Far more women go out to work even than in the heyday of the Cotton Mill. Gaps in income are opening up as private house building brings more prosperous incomers. Once, the children played out of doors (often there was no room for play indoors), and enjoyed a rural, idyllic childhood. Today they sit at their computers and televisions as often as they play out of doors, because of parental fears for their safety, and traffic danger in the streets.

There are many incomers in Blackburn today, but then it has always been a place where the population came and went, according to the work available. There is still deprivation today and some also perceive a loss of community spirit. Certainly the people have less in common with each other than once they had, but the extent of voluntary and community work in the societies, churches and clubs of the town surely proves that there are as many committed, hard-working volunteers with Blackburn's interests at heart as there have ever been.

So Blackburn has flourished, decayed, flourished again and decayed again, and is once more in a moderately flourishing period. With such a tumultuous history, the people of Blackburn have had to develop great resilience, fortitude and self-help. A very few of its families can perhaps trace their line right back to the old fermtoun of Blackburn, but today most Blackburn people are incomers, or descended from incomers. Without new blood, a community grows narrow and inward looking; and newcomers from a variety of backgrounds – Irish, English, Polish, Glaswegian, Asian, Chinese – have all contributed to the flavour, vigour and variety of Blackburn life. Many difficulties have been endured and overcome; Blackburn now looks set for a brighter future.

Appendix 1

Population of Blackburn

1794	'near 200'	(Old Statistical Account)
1841	443	
1851	684	
1861	758	
1871	954	(Groome's Ordnance Gazetteer)
1881	826	"
1891	814	"
1901	879	
1911	1,377	(Blackburn Special Drainage District)
1921	1,903	"
1931	2,022	"
1941	No census because of the war	
1951	3,354	
1961	4,302	(Blackburn Electoral Division)
1968	9,051	(WLCC estimate)
1971	7,632	
1981	5,786	
1991	5,042	
2001	4,761	
2005	4,988	

Appendix II

Timeline

1764	Turnpike Trust set up to build the Great Road
1769	George Moncrieff concludes his purchase of Blackburn
1770	'New Town' of Blackburn is begun
1770s	The old fermtoun of Blackburn moves to its new site
1772	Blackburn House built
1774	Blackburn Bridge built (Mill Road Bridge)
1793	Cotton Mill built
1803	William Kelly buys the Cotton Mill
1808	Robert Thom has become managing partner of the Cotton Mill by 1808
1822	Great Road straightened and new bridge built over Almond at west end
1823	James Sceales sets up flax works in Mill of Blackburn and Hopefield Mill
1824	Congregational chapel set up in Blackburn
c.1838	Church of Scotland sets up a chapel of ease
1840	The flax spinning and weaving works close down
1840s	New road built to connect Blackburn Cross with the West Calder Road
1846	Hopefield Mill converted to a grain mill & Mill of Blackburn to housing
1850s	First miners settle in Blackburn
1853	Robert Gilkison & Co. buy the Cotton Mill
1856	Cotton Mill workforce reaches its highest level – c.200
1860s	Crown Inn opens
1868	Hopefield Mill is converted from a grain mill to a paper mill
1872	Police Station built in Bathgate Road, near the Cross
c.1873–7	Livingston school board builds a public school in Kidd Street
1877	Cotton Mill destroyed by fire
1880	Cotton Mill building patched up and used as a paper mill
1880s	Coal mining becomes Blackburn's major employer
1891	Coal first produced at Riddochhill Colliery
	Establishment of a UP/UF mission
	West Calder Co-operative Society opens a branch in Blackburn
c. 1898	Present Almond Inn built
1899	The Turf opens
1900	Sinking of Whitrigg Pit begins
1905	Establishment of a Catholic parish covering Blackburn, Whitburn, etc.
1908	Sinking of the Lady Pit begins
	Blackburn UF Church opens
1911	Redhouse Public School opens
	Baillie Institute opens

1912	First Gala Day
1914	Lakestone quarry closes after some 75 years in operation
c.1916	Midland Moss Litter Co. begins to dig peat at Easter Inch Moss
1921	Miners' strike, April-July
1924	Catholic Church opens in West Main Street
1926	General Strike; miners remain out May-December
1927	First council houses
1929	Gospel Hall opens in the old village hall
1930s	RC school opens in the old public school in Kidd Street
	Old houses in Main Street demolished under 'slum clearance'
	Riddochhill housing scheme begun
1935	Blackburnhall Farm divided up into smallholdings
1936	Rev. John Lindsay gives the Lindsay Hall to the parish church
	Miners' Welfare Hall opens
1938	Pithead baths built at Riddochhill
1940s–50s	Riddochhill scheme completed; Mosside SSHA houses built
1945–46	Murrayfield Rovers FC undefeated, and win the Lord Weir Cup 1946–7
	Prefabs built in Ladeside Avenue
1947	Nationalisation of coal mines
1949	Blackburn becomes a Catholic parish on its own
	Tommy Miller wins several British boxing titles
1953	RC Primary School opens in Hopefield Road (Our Lady of Lourdes)
1954	Catholic Church burns down
1955	1,300 employed at Whitrigg
c.1956	Moss Litter operations cease
1956	Present Police Station opens
1959	Blackburn Primary School opens
	West Lothian county council agrees to take Glasgow overspill families
1960	British Motor Company comes to Bathgate
1961	First truck rolls off the line at BMC
	Consecration of the new Catholic Chapel in Bathgate Road
1960s	Murrayfield estate built
1962	Livingston New Town designated
1964	Murrayfield Primary School opens
	Almondvale Old People's Home opens
1965	First sites ready on Whitehill Industrial Estate
1966	Community centre opens
	Public library opens
	Shopping Centre opens
1967	National Commercial Bank (later the Royal Bank) opens
	Golden Hind Hotel opens
	Adult occupation centre opens

	Pinewood School opens
1968	Riddochhill Pit closes
1970	96 per cent public ownership of housing, and 4 per cent owner occupied
1972	Blackburn Academy opens
1970s/80s	Efforts to solve problems of Murrayfield estate
1971	British Leyland Social Club opens
1972	Whitrigg Pit closes
1973	St Kentigern's Academy opens
1976	First Gala Civic Week
	Masonic lodge (formerly the Lindsay Hall) opens
	Lothian regional council designation as an 'area of multiple deprivation'
1978	Blackburn United FC set up
1981	British Leyland Social Club closes
1984	Bield Sheltered Housing opens in Mosside Road
1985	Start of the Young Families Project
	Redhouse School closes
1986	Final closure of British Leyland
1988	No Gala Day
1992	Blackburn Academy closes
1994	Blackburn and Seafield Credit Union set up
1997	Royal Bank of Scotland closes its Blackburn branch
1999	Shopping Centre rebuilt and reopened as the Mill Centre
2000	Trinleyknowe Centre becomes the Blackburn Family Centre
2001	48 per cent public ownership of housing; 47 per cent owner occupied
2004	Community wardens appointed
2005	Work begins on restoration of Blackburn House

Gospel Hall

c.1800	Built as Village School
1838	Used by Church of Scotland as a chapel of ease
1877	Village Hall
1929	Becomes the Gospel Hall

Masonic Hall

c.1825	Built as Congregational chapel
1860s	Bought by Church of Scotland and used as chapel of ease
1890s	Bought by UF church and used until building of UF church, 1908
c.1914	Bought by Rev. John Lindsay and given to Blackburn UF/parish church
1936	Lindsay Hall
1976	Becomes the Masonic Hall

Further Reading

Alexander M. Bisset   *Episodes in West Lothian History*, Office of the *Linlithgowshire Gazette*, 1927

Stuart Borrowman   *Capital of Silicon Glen: West Lothian transformed for good?*, Drumduff Publications, 2000

Bill Cochrane   'The 1834 establishment of the Whitburn Penny Post Office at Blackburn' in *Scottish Post: the Journal of the Scottish Postal History Society*, No. 99, Autumn 2003

Ptolemy Dean   *Blackburn House, West Lothian, Scotland: Fourth Year Conservation Option, School of Architecture, University of Edinburgh*, 1990

William F. Hendrie   *Discovering West Lothian*, John Donald, 1986

Thomas Henney   *Murrayfield, Blackburn, General Improvements: a study of the effectiveness of community participation in environmental improvements*, 1979
Jubilee: Blackburn Church of Scotland 1908–58, Blackburn Parish Church, 1958

Thomas McNulty   *A Short History of Blackburn, 1905–1980*, Blackburn Catholic Church, 1981

Alex Russell   *Our Fault*, 2000

Jim Walker   *Jam Pieces, Galadays and Rock 'n' Roll*, Walker Kerr, 2001

West Lothian Council   *Blackburn – Local History: Sources for Primary Schools from the West Lothian Local History Library*, West Lothian Council Libraries, 2002

John Williams   *Journal of a mineral survey upon the estates of Sir W.A. Cunynghame, Bart., from Mid Calder to Polkemmet and from the foot of Breich Water to Hollisburn*, 1793

Index

Pumpherston: the story of a shale oil village

Sybil Cavanagh

ISBN 1 84282 015 X PBK £10.99
ISBN 1 84282 011 7 HBK £17.99

In 1884 the Pumpherston Oil Works was built and a substantial village came into being. The Pumpherston Oil Company is seen in the wider context of the shale oil industry. The story of its successes and failures is followed through the era of Scottish Oils and BP to the close-down of the shale oil industry in Scotland in 1962.

The village was built, supervised and patronised by the oil companies. A strange culture emerged in which the employers intervened in all aspects of their employees' lives, whether at work, at home or at leisure.

This fascinating book also looks at the rich social life that grew up in the village, and the wealth of characters – high achievers as well as eccentric worthies – that will stir the memories of everyone who grew up in or remembers Pumpherston in the old days.

And the story of Pumpherston comes full circle with the cleaning up of the oil works site. BP has used pioneering technology to clear the site of the pollution from more than a century of work, and to return the area to its original rural nature.

A rich mix of historical, technical and anecdotal material makes up a book that will appeal to readers not just in the local area, but to 'Pumphy' exiles all over the world and to anyone interested in the shale oil industry and Scotland's industrial heritage.

Linlithgow Life and Times

G W Lockhart

ISBN 1 905222 39 4 PBK £10.99

Why are inhabitants of Linlithgow known as 'Black Bitches'?
How did the Roke originate?
When did the hangman lead the Marches?

Whether you are a Black Bitch, an incomer or a visitor, this book has much to tell you about the captivating town of Linlithgow. It is steeped in history – it is the birthplace of Mary Queen of Scots, there in St Michael's Church James IV had his famous vision before leaving for defeat and death at Flodden, the Regent Moray fell to an assasin's bullet in its High Street and both Charles Edward Stuart and the Duke of Cumberland enjoyed at least a measure of hospitality in the most handsome of palaces.

But Linlithgow is not simply a historical footnote – it is today home to a vibrant and dynamic population, and hosts an array of clubs and societies. In *Linlithgow Life and Times*, Wallace Lockhart looks at the unique qualities of the town, and tells why he is proud to call himself an honorary Black Bitch. For visitors, this book will provide places of interest to visit and explore, while for locals it offers a chance to reflect on what makes Linlithgow such a special place – and perhaps learn a thing or two about their own town!

A wider population should be aware that beyond the palace and the traditions of which we are rightly proud, Linlithgow is today a vibrant community harbouring people from all over.
TAM DALYELL

Shale Voices

Alistair Findlay

ISBN 0 946487 63 4 PBK £10.99
ISBN 0 946487 78 2 HBK £17.99

Shale Voices offers a fascinating insight into shale mining, an industry that employed generations of Scots, had an impact on the social, political and cultural history of Scotland and gave birth to today's large oil companies. Author Alistair Findlay was born in the shale mining village of Winchburgh and is the fourth son of a shale miner, Bob Findlay, who became editor of the *West Lothian Courier*. *Shale Voices* combines oral history, local journalism and family history. The generations of communities involved in shale mining provide, in their own words, a unique documentation of the industry and its cultural and political impact. Photographs, drawings, poetry and short stories make this a thought provoking and entertaining account. It is much a joy to dip into and feast the eyes on as to read from cover to cover.

Alistair Findlay has added a basic source material to the study of Scottish History that is invaluable and will be of great benefit to future generations. Scotland owes him a debt of gratitude for undertaking this work.
TAM DALYELL

Hail Philpstoun's Queen... and other tales from the shale

Barbara and Marie Pattullo

ISBN 1 84282 094 X PBK £6.99

Mother and daughter team Barbara and Marie Pattullo take us back to the days of Rows houses and horse drawn grocers' vans, to summer gala days and thriving village sports clubs.

Back to a life of walking to school, coping with life at war so close to the Forth and socials at the village hall.

To a time when working life may have been hard but community spirit and village pride were well-founded.

It is that spirit, and that pride, that this book aims to record, and to honour.

I warmly applaud the authors for the skill with which they have woven into a verbal tapestry information they have gleaned from a variety of sources and, above all, for their assiduity in tracking down events and relationships which would otherwise be lost for ever.
TAM DALYELL

The Hydro Boys: pioneers of renewable energy

Emma Wood

ISBN 1 84282 047 8 PBK £8.99

 I heard about drowned farms and hamlets, the ruination of the salmon-fishing and how Inverness might be washed away if the dams failed inland. I was told about the huge veins of crystal they found when they were tunnelling deep under the mountains and when I wanted to know who 'they' were: what stories I got in reply! I heard about Poles, Czechs, poverty-stricken Irish, German spies, intrepid locals and the heavy drinking, fighting and gambling which went on in the NoSHEB contractors' camps.

Nobody should forget the human sacrifice made by those who built the dams all those years ago. The politicians, engineers and navvies of the era bequeathed to us the major source of renewable energy down to the present day. Their legacy will continue to serve us far into the 21st century.'
BRIAN WILSON MP, Energy Minister,
announcing a 'new deal for hydro' which now
'provides 50 per cent of the UK's renewable energy output. The largest generator serves more than 4 million customers.
THE SCOTSMAN

Bringing mains electricity to the Highlands and Islands did more for the area than anything else that's happened in my lifetime. This is the story of the people to whom we owe an awful lot. And what a great story it is.
JAMES HUNTER

Tunnel Tigers: a first-hand account of a Hydro Boy in the Highlands

Patrick Campbell

ISBN 1 84282 072 9 PBK £8.99

 Tunnel tigers belong to an elite group of construction workers who specialise in a highly paid but dangerous profession: driving tunnels through mountains or underneath rivers or other large bodies of water, on locations as far apart as Sydney, Australia, and San Francisco. At the turn of the last century, they tunnelled out the subways under New York and London; in the 1940s and 1950s, they were involved in a score of huge hydroelectric tunnels in Pitlochry and the Highlands of Scotland. They continue with their dangerous craft today in various locations all over the world.

Many of these daring men were born in north west Donegal, Ireland, where the tunnel tigers were viewed as local folk heroes because they had the bravado to work in dangerous working conditions that few other working men could endure.

Tunnel Tigers is a colourful portrait of the off-beat characters who worked on the Scottish projects, and of the tensions that were created when men of various religious and ethnic groups shared the same space.

Brilliant. Moving. Memorable... stories that stay with you for life.
CHRISTINE GOLDBECK

A poignant, gripping story.
HOWARD CROWN

Crofting Years

Francis Thompson

ISBN 0 946487 06 5 PBK £6.95

 Crofting is much more than a way of life in the Highlands and Islands of Scotland. It is a storehouse of cultural, linguistic and moral values, which holds together a scattered and struggling rural population. This book fills a blank in the written history of crofting over the last two centuries. Bloody conflicts and gunboat diplomacy, treachery, compassion, music and story: all figure as Francis Thompson takes us into the homes and the very minds of those who fought so desperately for security on their land.

I would recommend this book to all who are interested in the past, but even more so to those who are interested in the future survival of our way of life and culture.

STORNOWAY GAZETTE

A cleverly planned book... the story told in simple words which compel attention... [by] a Gaelic speaking Lewisman with specialised knowledge of the crofting community.

BOOKS IN SCOTLAND

An excellent social history of crofting in the Highlands and Islands by a writer with a deep knowledge of his subject.

THE SCOTS MAGAZINE

Reportage Scotland: Scottish history in the voices of those who were there

Louise Yeoman

ISBN 1 84282 051 6 PBK £7.99

 Events – both major and minor – as seen and recorded by Scots throughout history.

Which king was murdered in a sewer? What was Dr Fian's love magic?

Who was the half-roasted abbot?

Which cardinal was salted and put in a barrel?

Why did Lord Kitchener's niece try to blow up Burns's cottage?

The answers can all be found in the eclectic mix covering nearly 2000 years of Scottish history. Historian Louise Yeoman's rummage through the manuscript, book and newspapers archives of the National Library of Scotland has yielded an astonishing range of material from a letter to the king of the Picts to Mary Queen of Scots' own account of the murder of David Riccio; from the execution of William Wallace to accounts of anti-poll tax actions and the opening of the new Scottish Parliament. The book takes pieces from the original French, Latin, Gaelic and Scots and makes them accessible to the general reader, often for the first time.

The result is compelling reading for anyone interested in the history that has made Scotland what it is today.

Marvellously illuminating and wonderfully readable.

SCOTLAND ON SUNDAY

A monumental achievement in drawing together such a rich historical harvest.

THE HERALD

This City Now: Glasgow and its working class past

Ian R Mitchell

ISBN 1 84282 082 6 PBK £12.99

This City Now sets out to retrieve the hidden architectural, cultural and historical riches of some of Glasgow's working-class districts. Many who enjoy the fruits of Glasgow's recent gentrification will be surprised and delighted by the gems which Ian Mitchell has uncovered beyond the usual haunts.

An enthusiastic walker and historian, Mitchell invites us to recapture the social and political history of the working-class in Glasgow, by taking us on a journey from Partick to Rutherglen, and Clydebank to Pollokshaws, revealing the buildings which go unnoticed every day yet are worthy of so much more attention.

Once read and inspired, you will never be able to walk through Glasgow in the same way again.

... both visitors and locals can gain instruction and pleasure from this fine volume... Mitchell is a knowledgable, witty and affable guide through the streets of the city...
GREEN LEFT WEEKLY

Spectacles, Testicles, Fags and Matches: the untold story of RAF Servicing Commandos in World War II

Tom Atkinson

ISBN 1 84282 071 0 PBK £12.99

Spectacles, testicles, fags and matches was a ritual used by Servicing Commandos after doing anything they called 'hairy'. It was a completely non-religious act, but strangely comforting.

From the jungles of Burma to the foggy plains of Germany, the RAF Servicing Commandos were the men who kept the most advanced aircraft of the RAF flying. Yet there has been very little written about them. Historians, up to today, are surprised to learn of their existence and astonished to learn of their activities. But without those Units the RAF would have had great difficulty in providing close cover for the forward troops and the fighter planes would have spent less time in action.

These elite Units serviced and maintained, re-armed and re-fuelled, repaired and recovered the front line aircraft on which so much depended, and did it all immediately behind the most forward troops. Fully trained in the techniques of Combined Operations they could land from the seas on any hostile territory and establish new airstrips almost instantaneously. Equipped to be highly mobile, and to defend themselves and their airstrips, they would be ready to service the fighter squadrons within minutes, and service them quicker than they had ever been serviced before.

They are, surprisingly, the Forgotten Men. This is their story told by the men themselves.

Luath Press Limited
committed to publishing well written books worth reading

LUATH PRESS takes its name from Robert Burns, whose little collie Luath (*Gael.,* swift or nimble) tripped up Jean Armour at a wedding and gave him the chance to speak to the woman who was to be his wife and the abiding love of his life. Burns called one of 'The Twa Dogs' Luath after Cuchullin's hunting dog in Ossian's Fingal. Luath Press grew up in the heart of Burns country, and now resides a few steps up the road from Burns' first lodgings in Edinburgh's Royal Mile.

Luath offers you distinctive writing with a hint of unexpected pleasures.

Most UK and US bookshops either carry our books in stock or can order them for you. To order direct from us, please send a £sterling cheque, postal order, international money order or your credit card details (number, address of cardholder and expiry date) to us at the address below. Please add post and packing as follows: UK – £1.00 per delivery address; overseas surface mail – £2.50 per delivery address; overseas airmail – £3.50 for the first book to each delivery address, plus £1.00 for each additional book by airmail to the same address. If your order is a gift, we will happily enclose your card or message at no extra charge.

Luath Press Limited
543/2 Castlehill
The Royal Mile
Edinburgh EH1 2ND
Scotland
Telephone: 0131 225 4326 (24 hours)
Fax: 0131 225 4324
email: sales@luath.co.uk
Website: www.luath.co.uk

ILLUSTRATION: IAN KELLAS